Copyright ©℗ 2000 by Great American Audio Corporation
Cover Copyright © 2000 by Great American Audio Corporation
Book Design Copyright © 2000 Great American Audio Corporation
Published by Great American Audio Corporation, New Rochelle, NY 10801

ISBN: 07413-0038-9   49600BK

Manufactured in China

First Edition

10   9   8   7   6   5   4   3   2   1

Contents

Introduction ii

Chapter 1: The Beginning 1

Chapter 2: Mystery, Adventure, Horror, Suspense, Westerns 11

Chapter 3: Comedy 19

Chapter 4: Music Programs 29

Chapter 5: Popular Children's Programming 31

Chapter 6: Daytime Programming for the Ladies 35

Chapter 7: Panel, Quiz and Talk Shows 41

Chapter 8: Radio News Brings World War II Home 45

Chapter 9: Unforgettable Radio Moments 49

Chapter 10: The Golden Age of Radio Lives On 53

Program Notes 55

Index 61

Introduction

In an age when everybody has a personal website, and there is cable television programming aimed exclusively at fishermen, shopaholics and country-music fans, it may be hard to imagine a time when network radio created a feeling of community across the United States.

Yet that is exactly what happened. No, not everyone agreed on what to listen to. So-called highbrow programs, offering everything from classical drama to symphonic music, competed against lowbrow comedies and soap operas. But the choices were fewer then, and the audience wasn't nearly as fragmented as it is today. Someone who mentioned a gag from the Sunday night Jack Benny show at work on Monday was likely to get a chorus of responses. Millions of people were in the habit of tuning in Benny every week, and stuck with that habit for more than twenty years.

It's often been said that in the heyday of Amos 'n' Andy one could walk down the street of an American town on a summer night and follow the program as the sound drifted out of one house after another. Radio exerted a tremendous hold on Americans in the 1920's, 30's and 40's. The medium is still potent, but nowadays people tend to listen to radio while doing something else - shaving, driving the car, preparing a meal.

In that golden era, however, people actually listened. It wasn't just "television without pictures" because, as someone once said, the pictures were better on radio: you created them yourself. Radio not only invited but demanded participation on the part of the listener, and fired the most powerful tool of all:

the imagination.

Thus, when Jack Benny's echoing footsteps descended into his private vault, we pictured the scene in our mind.

When Sam Spade described a beautiful woman, we all created a vision of her–and each listener's "picture" was different.

And when Charlie McCarthy uttered one of his wisecracks, we were certain they were coming from his own mouth, even though logic told us that it was really Edgar Bergen doing the talking.

I've tried to listen to vintage radio shows scientifically, aloof from the emotional pull of the programs. It never works. As hard as I try to picture actors in front of a microphone in a barren studio, I find myself drifting into the scene they conjure up. Before long, I'm not seeing Jack Webb in shirtsleeves with a script in his hands; I'm thinking about Joe Friday running down clues on the streets of Los Angeles.

Sometimes it's the ambiance of the program that does the job: Gunsmoke, an extraordinarily atmospheric show from the twilight years of network radio comes to mind. The director, Norman Macdonnell, and his sound artists worked tirelessly to create a believable setting for their weekly western dramas. Sometimes it's the powerful writing that builds a mystique for the listener, as in the heightened prose of Norman Corwin and the sinuous storytelling of Arch Oboler or Carlton E. Morse. Corwin painted rich word pictures, while Oboler and Morse (especially on I Love A Mystery) spun wildly fanciful tales. Often it's the intimacy of the performances - so

immediate and real–that focus our imagination. Great radio actors like Elliott Lewis, Jeanette Nolan, Hans Conried, Raymond Edward Johnson, Agnes Moorehead, and Lurene Tuttle (to name just a few) imbued every role they played with two equally important ingredients: truth and color. They were never dull.

If radio was stimulating for its audience, imagine what it must have been like for participants. Here was a truly collaborative medium in which actors sat side by side with sound-effect artists, musicians, writers, directors and engineers. There wasn't the caste system that existed in movies or the compartmentalization that developed in television, in which a composer might never meet the writer of the show he was scoring and the sound technicians would be discouraged from mingling with the stars. Partly because it was done "live," with no margin for error, radio demanded teamwork and that in turn bred camaraderie unique in show business history. No wonder so many radio veterans speak so fondly of their work in this medium. Truth be told, not everything about the "Golden Age of Radio" was golden. With hours to fill, seven days a week, and no such thing as reruns, radio had more than its share of drivel: simplistic soap operas, hackneyed juvenile adventures, and hokey comedies were a dime a dozen. Musical shows were so eager for new material that they pounced on a promising new song and bled it dry within a matter of weeks. And yet… there was room for experimentation. There were "prestige" programs never intended to make a dime …and thoughtful shows that had a profound influence on American society.

"Sustaining programs" were aired without commercials - both to fill time and fulfill the FCC mandate to provide programming in the public interest. In this rarefied atmosphere such outsized talents as Orson Welles, Irving Reis and Norman Corwin flourished. Arturo Toscanini conducted the NBC Symphony without fear of audience share or rating points.

Even in the commercial world the sheer variety of sponsors enabled shows as varied as Fibber McGee and Molly and The Voice of Firestone to coexist. Orson Welles later reckoned that this was the biggest single difference between radio, in which sponsors were responsible for programming and television, which evolved into a handful of firestorms in which a few network executives determined the fate of all programming.

I love listening to old-time radio… not just the "quality" shows but the bread and butter serials like The Lone Ranger and Sergeant Preston of the Yukon. How can a grown man get so involved in such formulaic predictable stories? One might ask why anyone who's seen Carmen or LaTraviata would want to sit through another performance. The answer is plain in both cases: it's not the destination but the journey that's so much fun.

My wife and I even got our daughter hooked, when she was quite young. While driving in the car, we put on the Jack Benny show and at the age of four, she immediately latched onto the silliness of Dennis Day. In time, she grew to love the entire Benny cast and still looks forward to each new episode we play.

Perhaps when the children of tomorrow grow tired of visual stimulation and virtual reality, they will find refuge in the simplicity of radio. After all, it inspired George Lucas, who went on to create "Star Wars." What better poster boy could there be for radio, and its power to stir the imagination?

Biography of Leonard Maltin

Leonard Maltin first wrote about Walt Disney in a special edition of his magazine Film Fan Monthly *in 1967, which in turn led to the first edition of his book* Disney Films. *He is also the author of* Mice and Magic: A History of American Animated Cartoons. *But he is perhaps best known for his annual paperback reference,* Leonard Maltin's Movie and Video Guide, *which he has edited since 1969. Since 1982 he has been commentator and interviewer on television's "Entertainment Tonight," and is currently film critic for* Playboy Magazine.

He also hosts a daily syndicated radio feature, and appears regularly on the Encore cable TV service. His other books include Leonard Maltin's Movie Encyclopedia, The Great American Broadcast, The Great Movie Comedians, The Disney Films, Of Mice and Magic: A History of American Animated Cartoons, The Art of the Cinematographer, Selected Short Subjects, *and as co-author of* The Little Rascals: Life and Times of Our Gang. *His articles have appeared in* Satellite Direct, Modern Maturity, The New York Times, The Los Angeles Times Premiere, Smithsonian, TV Guide, Esquire, The Village Voice *and* Disney Magazine.

He has served as guest curator at the Museum of Modern Art, was a member of the faculty of the New School for Social Research and was President of the Los Angeles Film Critics Association in 1995 and 1996. In 1997 he was named to the national Film Preservation Board and in 1998 he began teaching at the University of Southern California.

Leonard Maltin is the author of numerous books including *The Great American Broadcast: A Celebration of Radio's Golden Age (Dutton)*. His annual paperback reference *Leonard Maltin's Movie & Video Guide* is a perennial best-seller, but perhaps he is best known as the longtime film correspondent on television's "Entertainment Tonight."

"Return with us now to those thrilling days of yesteryear…"

…*when everyone in America knew who that "masked man" was, that "crime did not pay," the names of the couple who lived at 79 Wistful Vista, they listened to "tales well calculated to keep [them] in suspense" and were convinced that Lux was "the soap of the stars," not to mention the answer to feminine "daintiness." Why?*

Because they were listening to The Shadow, The Lone Ranger, Fibber McGee and Molly, Suspense, and The Lux Radio Theater on the big radio that occupied the place of pride in their living rooms. RADIO as it used to be, when people still believed that mom, apple pie, chicken soup, and the Republic, could get them through anything from the common cold to two world wars. This was a time when radio was an important player in the world of information and entertainment.

CHAPTER ONE

The Beginning

The Beginning

Senetore Guglielmo Marconi
was a frequent speaker over the networks of the National Broadcasting Company. He is shown here during his last visit to the United States, as he spoke on NBC from his suite at the Ritz-Carlton Hotel in New York.

Before the inventions of the telephone, telegraph, and radio, people could only communicate with each other over great distances by the written word via mail, or the printed word via news publications, magazines and books, not always readily available to all and limited as to the timeliness of their information. Pens, printing devices, ink, literacy, and the time it took to transport messages did not make for speedy communication. But the inventions of the telephone and telegraph cut that time down to just about instant. Radio waves could carry sound to distant places and be heard by people far away almost immediately. For people living across a vast, sprawling nation like America–or across a continent like Europe–it was astounding, though not exactly unexpected.

The idea of long-distance communication without written words had been around since the early 1800's, when scientists Joseph Henry and Michael Faraday first theorized that an electric current traveling over one wire could produce a current in another wire. A paper published by James Clerk Maxwell in 1864 stated that light waves were electromagnetic waves containing electric and magnetic fields.

Then when Henrich Hertz used this information to send and receive radio waves (just noise) in the 1880's, the transmission of more meaningful sound (e.g. Morse code, a series of short and long beeps and blips–visually dots and dashes–representing the letters of the alphabet) became a very real possibility. It did not occur to Hertz, however, that electromagnetic waves could be heard over great distances--across the Atlantic between Europe and North America, for example. This was left to the man now known as "the Father of modern radio"–Guglielmo Marconi. In 1895, Marconi produced a wireless telegraph sound system using Hertz's ideas. Although he was an Italian, it was the British government that granted Marconi his first "wireless" patent. Marconi believed that the distance sound waves were transmitted could be greatly increased by the height of antennas or aerials.

In March 1899, the very first wireless messages were sent across the English Channel to the European continent. Two years later, on December 12, 1901, the first transatlantic message was sent, using the aforementioned Morse code, from Cornwall on the West Coast

of England to St. John's in Newfoundland in North America. In 1906, physicist Reginald Aubrey Fessenden sent a message using his voice from Brant Rock, Massachusetts, to ships in the middle of the Atlantic Ocean, but the sound, though human, was nearly inaudible.

The march toward radio as we now know it took a major step when Sir Ambrose Fleming developed the electron tube in 1907. Fleming's tube made the detection of high-frequency radio waves, and the sound of voice broader and more definitive. The audiontube, invented by Lee De Forest, allowed radio and sound waves to be amplified, and suddenly, we were transmitting voices distinctly and understandably human, if not quite as realistic as our own. However, until radio receivers had been improved to make listening better, radio was only of minor, if any, interest to the American public. But in 1918, that changed when Edwin Armstrong developed his superheterodyne circuit, which mixed incoming signals using fixed frequencies, therefore clarifying the sounds heard over the airwaves. This fixed frequency amplified the information being received, made more lifelike sound possible, and modern day radio was born.

1895

Marconi produces a wireless telegraph sound system

1899

First wireless message sent across the English Channel to the European continent

1901

First transatlantic message was sent using the aforementioned Morse code

1907

Sir Ambrose Fleming develops the electron tube

The First Radio Broadcasts

Nobody knows for sure what the first radio broadcast was, but it is known that an enterprising gentleman named Dr. Frank Conrad set up a local radio station in the garage of his home in Pittsburgh, Pennsylvania in 1920. His home-studio was a simple affair, and his broadcast schedule consisted of brief announcements of local events and recorded music. He was financed by the Westinghouse Electric and Manufacturing Company of Pittsburgh, which employed him as an assistant chief engineer and believed that he was on to something on which they might later be able to capitalize. Conrad's broadcasting station was given the call letters KDKA, in order to distinguish it from future wireless activities. (The smart money knew this fledgling would grow.) The first radio commercial, of a sort, was heard when Conrad reported that the records heard on his local station had been purchased at the local Joseph Horne Company Department Store in Pittsburgh.

When an article in The Pittsburgh Sun newspaper appeared saying that radio receivers could be purchased at the Horne Store for "as little as $10," interest in the media began to soar. Fortunately, the signals sent out by KDKA could be heard not only in the Pittsburgh area, but also in nearby West Virginia and Eastern Ohio. Soon thousands of people were talking about the incredible new "talking box"–radio. It didn't take long for the rest of America to become interested in the new invention which not only gave them "free" music over the airwaves, but also the latest news and exciting, on-the-spot events such as President Warren Harding's inauguration ceremony address, the Jess Willard-Luis Firpo boxing match, church-service broadcasts, speeches by presidential contender Herbert Hoover, and a live

broadcast of music performed by Gill's Orchestra, with vocal selections by Miss Ada Frances and Mr. Red Ward. Piano accompaniment for these musical interludes was provided by Miss Julia Barletti of the Pittsburgh Community Chorus.

The public's reaction was positive. Other stations began to surface rapidly as Westinghouse realized that interest in this new form of entertainment/communication warranted an expansion of their broadcasting activities. WWJ, a Detroit news station, and WJZ in Newark, New Jersey, were two of the new stations created by Westinghouse. WBZ in East Springfield, Massachusetts and KYW in Chicago, soon followed, as Westinghouse realized it could increase its sales of radio receivers wherever their advertisements could be heard. It didn't take long for other companies to recognize radio's commercial potential and soon companies such as General Electric, AT&T and the Radio Corporation of America (RCA) were opening stations of their own. By 1923, over 200 licenses to operate radio stations had been issued by the Federal Government. It decided it had better begin to regulate the broadcasting industry before all sorts of "undesirable" things began to be heard over the airwaves.

Radio Becomes A National Rage

As performers realized how many people were "tuned in" to radio broadcasts, entertainers like orchestra leader Paul Whiteman and vaudeville comedian Ed "The Perfect Fool" Wynn decided they might be able to increase the size of their audiences by performing "on radio" for thousands, instead of a mere hundreds of fans. Wynn was heard on one of the first important, well-publicized, aired-live comedy shows, presented by WJZ

in the New York City area, in 1922. His appearance on this show created a sensation, the talk of show business. When he realized just how popular radio had become, Wynn decided to broadcast on a regular basis, becoming one of radio's first major stars. **The Ed Wynn Show** (later called **The Fire Chief**, and sponsored by the Texaco Oil Company) became a staple on radio well into the 1930's. Orchestra leader Paul Whiteman, well known as "The King of Jazz," and already world-famous for his concert performances of George Gershwin's "Rhapsody in Blue" and other Swing and Jazz Age music, jumped on the radio bandwagon and began to be heard regularly on WJZ .

Radios Anyone Could Afford

Radio's first home receiver was a clumsy-looking machine called "the wireless," and could only be heard by donning an individual headset (earphones). Later receivers had internal speakers which amplified sound, making earphones unnecessary. They were transformed into handsome pieces of wooden furniture, now considered works of art worthy of exhibition by the Museum of Modern Art in New York City. RCA, Westinghouse and General Electrical began to mass-produce radios as fascination with the new medium grew. First came the cathedral-shaped radios, so identified with old-time radio. Then the rectangular art deco table-top radios and, most importantly perhaps, the large wooden console radios. These occupied a prominent place in our parlors or living rooms, the hearts of our homes, where families gathered to hear the wonderful entertainment and latest news items, previously only available in print, or in gathering places outside the home such as theaters, public dance halls, or sports arenas.

1918

Edwin Armstrong developed the superheterodyne circuit

1920

Dr. Frank Conrad set up a local radio station in the garage of his home in Pittsburgh, Pennsylvania

1923

Over 200 licenses to operate radio stations had been issued

Radio Stars Begin to Shine

As the number of famous performers that found their way to radio increased, so did the number of people who bought radio receivers to hear them. Listening to the home radio became a national pastime. Besides Wynn and Whiteman, such performers as contralto Vaughn De Leath, singer Irene Bordoni, **The Happiness Boys**, classical-music commentator Milton Cross, Broadway stars Julia Sanderson and Frank Crumit, **The Cliquot Club Eskimo Orchestra**, and The **A&P Gypsies** kept audiences near those dials. But there were three giants who turned radio from a cozy compulsion into a national craze, and whose fame, in turn, was increased enormously by the listening phenomena itself. They were crooner Rudy Vallee, soprano Jessica Dragonette, and Ziegfield Follies star and down-home humorist Will Rogers.

Vaughn De Leath made her radio debut in 1920. She had a deep, rich contralto voice which critics said was "a voice perfectly suited for the microphone."

She remained a radio favorite well into the 1930's, often billed herself as "The Original Radio Girl," and was a frequent guest on the renowned **Voice of Firestone** music program in the 1930's. The Happiness Boys (Billy Jones and Ernie Hare), a close-harmony singing duet, were an instant success from their first aired song in 1921. Their popularity continued into the 1930's.

Also known as The Interwoven Pair (the company name of an early sponsor), the duet had originally been heard on WJZ where they introduced such song hits as "Side By Side" and "The Two of Us Together." Their theme song, "How Do You Do," was well known to millions of radio's earliest listeners.

Soprano Irene Bordoni was the star of **The Coty Program** and **The RKO Hour** in the late 1920's. She had a large and loyal listening audience, and introduced such saucy songs as "It's A Lovely

Day Tomorrow" and "Let's Do It." Bordoni also remained popular into the mid-30's, when she retired from the airwaves.

The Cliquot Club Eskimo Orchestra starred on one of radio's most popular shows of the same name, and enjoyed a large listening audience from 1926 until 1936. The orchestra featured banjoist Harry Reser as its leader, and included Raymond Knight, Merle Johnson, Jimmy Brierly and Everett Clark, the Six Jumping Jacks, Loretta Clemens, Speed Young and Virginia Heyer. They were sponsored by the Cliquot Club Company. An orchestra that everyone remembers, if only for their name, was the A&P Gypsies. Led by Harry Horlick, it first aired in 1924. Sponsored by the A&P food company, the show's theme song, "Two Guitars," became a best-selling record and song sheet in the mid-20's because of its on-the-air exposure.

Radio Programming in the 1920's

At the time celebrities Ed Wynn and Paul Whiteman were making forays into radio, unknowns and semi-professionals were performing on the relatively few stations that existed. The Friday, September 12, 1924, log of programs presented on the AT&T station, WEAF in New York City, illustrates the breadth of early radio programming.

"Heigh-ho, everybody!" **Rudy Vallee**

11:00 a.m. – Helen Morris, soprano
11:10 a.m. – Health Talk by Dr. William St. Lawrence (Association for the Prevention of Heart Disease)
11:25 a.m. – The Flower Garden's Big Opportunity (Leonard Barron, Editor of Garden Magazine and Home Builder)
11:50 a.m. – Consolidated Market and Weather Report
4-5:00 p.m. – Woman's Club Program
6:00 p.m. – Dinner Music from the Rose Room of the Hotel Waldorf-Astoria in New York City (Joseph Knecht, conductor)
7:00 p.m. – "Sir Hobgoblin Broadcasts a Get-Up Time Story" (G.R. Kinney and Company Story Teller)
7:45 p.m. – Harry Jentes, Jazz pianist
7:55 p.m. – Rosalie Sheiner, 10 year old vocalist
8:05 p.m. – Isabel Duff "Scotty" Wood, soprano Program of Scottish Songs
8:20 p.m. – Harry Jentes, Jazz pianist
8:35 p.m. – Joseph White, tenor
8:50 p.m. – Rosalie Sheiner, 10 year old vocalist
9-10:00 p.m. – B. Fischer and Company, Astor Coffee Dance Orchestra
10:00 p.m. – Joseph White, tenor
10-11:00 p.m. – Special Radio Program on National Defense Test Day

Top Rated

Twenty years before Frank Sinatra and ten years before Bing Crosby became singing sensations, crooner Rudy Vallee was the most popular male vocalist in America. In the 1920's, Rudy became famous as "The Vagabond Lover" (a tribute to his casual, devil-may-care attitude), and his voice made ladies of all ages swoon with delight. Vallee was already a supper-club sensation when he took to the airwaves and his nasal voice introduced such top-ten hits as "The Whiffenpoof Song," "My Time Is Your Time," and "Blue Moon." His singing and college-boy looks led to film appearances. He remained in the spotlight for over forty years. Vallee's popular radio program, **The Fleischmann Hour**, remained one of radio's most popular programs from 1929 until 1939.

Jessica Dragonette's performances on **The Cities Service Concerts, Saturday Night Serenade** and **The Palmolive Beauty Box Show** made this attractive soprano one of the most famous women in America. Each week, millions of listeners tuned in to hear the soprano, called "the Greta Garbo of the airwaves," sing their favorite songs from musical comedies, operas, and operettas, as well as current song hits. Some believed her memorable name contributed to her fame. The homespun humor and easy-going, conversational style of Vaudeville and Broadway star, Will Rogers, proved perfect for the intimacy of the family living room. Each week, from the 1920's through the mid-1930's, listeners tuned in to hear Roger's rural wit and wisdom on such shows as **The Eveready Hour** and **The Ziegfeld Follies of the Air**. He remained one of radio's brightest stars until his untimely death in an airplane crash in 1935.

Amos 'n' Andy Arrive

In 1929, a program made its debut that became one of radios longest-running, most beloved, and memorable shows **Amos 'n' Andy**. Amos 'n' Andy was the first situation comedy developed specifically for radio. The title characters were two black men who lived in Manhattan and owned "The Fresh Air Taxi Company," with one dilapidated cab in its "fleet." Two white actors, Freeman Gosden and Charles Correll, played the parts of Amos 'n' Andy. Both had created these roles on radio, in 1926, using the names of Sam and Henry. When the newly formed NBC network picked up the series, the characters' names were changed to Amos and Andy in order to avoid any legal problems with the local station that had first aired the show. For almost thirty years, Amos 'n' Andy delighted listeners across America. In the early 1930's, the show was so popular, motion-picture-theater owners interrupted whatever film they were showing and turned on their radios so that the audience in the theater could listen to their weekly Amos 'n' Andy episode without staying home. By the time Amos 'n' Andy left the air in 1960, their funny, con-artist pal, George "The Kingfish" Stevens (also played by Freeman Gosden), had become the program's central character. Over the years, Amos 'n' Andy was most memorably sponsored by Rexall Drugs and Rinso Cleanser. Its theme songs were "The Perfect Song," and "Angel's Seranade." Amos 'n' Andy was just the beginning of what was to become "The Golden Age of Radio." Much of the very best was yet to come.

Will Rogers
America's first political satirist.

Amos 'n' Andy
George Bernard Shaw gave them their finest tribute when he said "There are three things I'll never forget about America: The Rocky Mountains, Niagara Falls, and Amos and Andy."

William S. Paley, CBS President

David Sarnoff, the hard driving immigrant from Russia, started as an office boy for the Marconi Company and quickly rose to the head of the most powerful communications company on earth.

The National Broadcasting Company (NBC)

In 1919, the General Electric Company, with The Radio Corporation of America (RCA) as one of its subsidiary companies, acquired the Marconi Wireless Telegraph Company of America from a British-owned company. At the time, Marconi Wireless was the only company handling commercial transatlantic radio communications. For the next fifty years, RCA's radio operations were led by David Sarnoff, who built the company into one of the largest communications conglomerates in the world. In 1928, RCA formed the National Broadcasting Company to manage its national network of local stations and their ever-growing radio activities. Fearing that a network might become too large and powerful, the Federal government formed the Federal Communications Commission (FCC) in order to protect the public in a variety of ways; for example, preventing broadcasting companies from presenting too many commercial messages. By 1941, the National Broadcasting Company, by now enormous, owned two separate networks of stations, the Blue Network and the Red Network. The FCC, wanting to discourage monopolies in the broadcasting industry, demanded that RCA (NBC) sell one of its two networks of stations. NBC obliged and sold their Blue network to businessman Edward J. Noble in 1943.

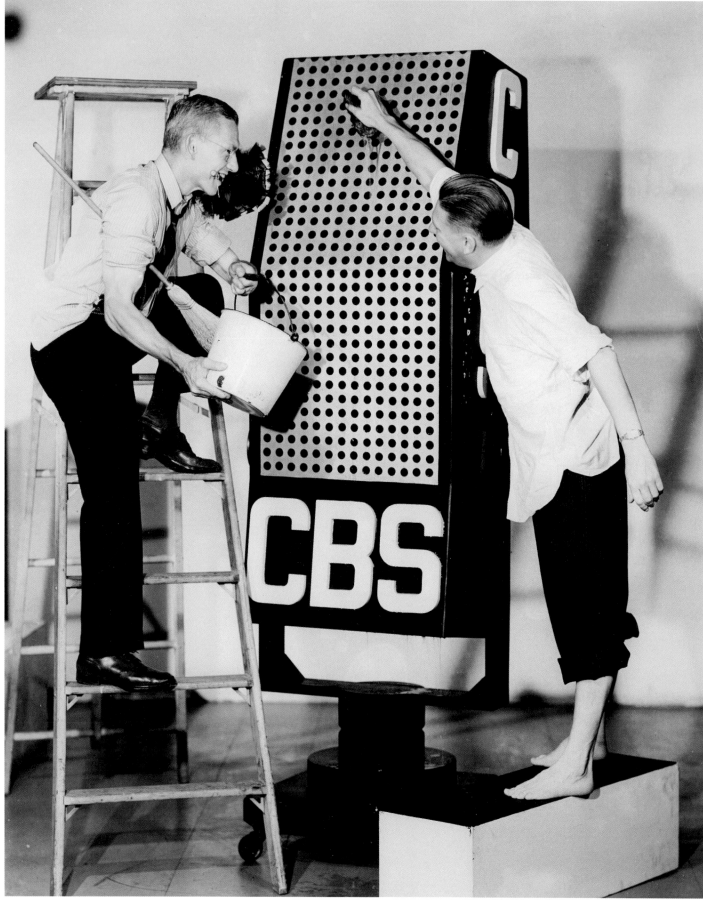

The Columbia Broadcasting System (CBS)

In 1926, an ambitious young businessman, named William S. Paley, bought several local radio stations in order to advertise his father's tobacco company products. Paley called his new group of radio stations The United Independent Broadcasters. As the company prospered, Paley changed its name to the Columbia Broadcasting System (which sounded more like the already successful National Broadcasting Company), and bought several more stations. The clever young businessman attracted a great deal of attention in the business world as he actively began to compete for advertisers with the powerful NBC. Paley offered advertisers a wider audience for their products by delivering commercial messages over a broader area via several of his network's stations, rather than just advertising local products to local customers. It didn't take long for Columbia (CBS) to become NBC's major broadcasting competitor. Soon Paley realized that the key to making even greater profits was to offer free programming to affiliate stations in return for having a certain percentage of their schedule devoted to shows produced by CBS. For a network to produce its own programs was a revolutionary idea. NBC soon followed suit.

Arthur Sears Henning, *one of the Mutual Radio Network's 1940 convention newscaster*

The Mutual Broadcasting System (MBS)

Formed in 1934, when four privately owned Eastern and Midwestern radio stations (WGN in Chicago, WOR in New York City, WLW in Cincinnati, and WXYZ in Detroit) decided to form a network of their own to compete with the super powerful National Broadcasting Company. Unlike NBC and CBS, Mutual never had central ownership, but each station produced programs, which were made available to their sister-stations. Because their creative departments were able to produce such popular shows as The Lone Ranger, The Shadow and Nick Carter, their profits soon began to soar. The company was dissolved in the early 1960's and each of its affiliated stations resumed their individual activities.

Abbott and Costello Show *with guest star Turham Bey*

The American Broadcasting Company (ABC)

A year after NBC sold their Blue network in 1943 to Edward J. Noble, owner of the Life Savers Candy Company, its name was changed to the American Broadcasting Company. Noble wanted to make his new network of stations a "quality" operation. For many years, he held the reins of his company tightly and refused to allow daytime serials, for example, to be heard on his network, convinced that these programs were overly romantic and sentimental trash. He preferred that ABC is known for such fare as classical music and dramatic anthology shows. Shortly after, commercial pressures forced Noble and his business into similar programming as NBC and CBS.

NBC's Studios. "Truth or Consequences" Program, New York City, May 1942

Radio's Golden Age

From the early 1930's until 1960, years now known as The Golden Age of Radio, the public was offered an increasingly varied menu of programs—mysteries, variety shows, situation comedies, dramatic anthology programs, soap operas, children's adventure serials, panel and game shows, music shows, talk, information and news programs. Although it is difficult for most of today's kids to imagine, during the Great Depression (1929 until the late 1930's), unemployment was rampant and money so tight, even the nickel price of a ticket to a movie theater cut too deeply into the food and rent budget. But the radio, if you were lucky enough to own one from better times—and lots of folks did—offered free entertainment for the entire family,

momentary escape from the difficult times in which they were living. Even during later bad times.

During World War II, for example, radio became an important escape mechanism. "Blackouts" were ordered, at which time all the lights, including every home light, in a community had to be turned out, so that enemy Nazi or Japanese planes would not be able to seek out targets to bomb. Families would gather, as during earlier hard times, around the living room radio and pass a dark, but not so forbidding evening together because of the radio. It was during this time that people began talking about "the theater of the mind" a phrase that described the special and positive experience of listening to the radio. Instead of seeing the same image as everybody else as on a stage or on a movie screen, listeners found they could "picture" whatever it was they were hearing in their own

unique ways. Radio's heroes and heroines were handsome or beautiful in the way each listener wanted them to be, that is, beyond the ability of anyone else to visually create. Scary narratives became more terrifying in the mind than they could ever be on a screen or stage. Funny jokes and situations often seemed funnier than the description of what was really going on. Silences, like the legendary long pause on one of Jack Benny's shows, had the listening audience, who could not have known what was going on, howling with laughter at something only they could know. It was the longest pause—followed by the longest laugh—in show business. In short, radio allowed people to use their imaginations—and they loved every minute of it.

Mystery, Adventure, Horror, Suspense, Westerns

Mystery, Adventure, Horror, Suspense, Westerns

The Shadow

The Shadow (1930-1954) is probably the radio show most people think of first when asked to recall the name of a famous mystery program. It was originally heard on radio in 1930 with actor Jack La Curto playing Lamont Cranston, alias The Shadow. While in the Orient, Cranston had learned the "power to cloud men's minds," making him invisible when he wanted to be. He used this ability to fight crime, claiming "the weed of crime bears bitter fruit… crime does not pay!" The program opened with the Shadow asking:

"Who knows what evil lurks in the hearts of men? The Shadow knows!" He then uttered a sinister laugh; unforgettable to anyone who ever heard it. Over the years, several actors played The Shadow, including Orson Welles, but it was Bret Morrison who played the character longest. He was the last to play the Shadow, and the Cranston/Shadow voice people remember best. For many years, The Shadow was sponsored by the Blue Coal Company. By the time it went off the air in 1954, its theme song. Omphale's Spinning Wheel, was as familiar to listeners as the show itself.

"Who knows what evil lurks in the hearts of men…

Orson Welles as **The Shadow**

Because they were especially suited to radio, mystery and crime programs outnumbered most of the other types of shows heard on the air. Murder, mayhem, and something about the atmosphere, mostly dark and more than a little scary, did, indeed, lend itself easily to that "theater of the mind." While there were many original characters created just for radio, famous detectives from film and literature also found their way to the airwaves. Among the hundreds of mystery/crime shows, audience favorites were: **The Adventures of Charlie Chan** *(1932-1948)*, starring Walter Connolly, Santos Ortega, and Ed Begley as the celebrated Chinese-Hawaiian detective at different times; **The Adventures of Ellery Queen** *(1939-1948)* featuring several actors (most memorably Hugh Marlowe) in the title role. Before the show was over, famous guest panelists, as well as the listening audience, were given all the clues, and a chance to solve the mystery themselves, before Ellery revealed all; **The Adventures of Mr. and Mrs. North** *(1942-1955)*, which during its most listened-to years, starred actress Alice Frost and actor Joseph Curtin as the husband and wife sleuths, was a kind of update to Nick and

Nora Charles of The Thin Man; **The Adventures of Philip Marlowe** *(1947-1951)* starring actor Gerald Mohr as the tough-talking, no-nonsense private eye, Marlowe, was part of our love affair with mystery writer Raymond Chandler; **Richard Diamond, Private Detective** *(1949-1953)*, with film star Dick Powell as the wise-cracking, hard-boiled detective, always sang a song, in the inimitable Powell style, at the end of each show; **The Adventures of Sam Spade, Detective** *(1946-1951)* starred actor Howard Duff as Spade, created by Dashiell Hammett, and probably the most famous hard-boiled, smart-mouthed PI of all time. Lurene Tuttle played his secretary, Effie Perrine, a.k.a. "Angel." Spade's weekly "capers" and his private detective badge number, 137596, were very familiar throughout the country; **The Adventures of Sherlock Holmes** *(1930-1956)* was most popular when the series starred screen actors Basil Rathbone and Nigel Bruce, recreating their film roles as Holmes and Dr. Watson in the radio adaptations of Arthur Conan Doyle's stories; **The Adventures of the Thin Man** *(1941-1942)* starred Claudia Morgan and Les Damon as the sophisticated couple who had a talent for stumbling upon murders. Despite all efforts at imitation, the couple, also created by Dashiell Hammett, remained very distinct from the Norths (audiences loved them both); and **Big Town** *(1937-1952)* originally starred the silver screen's Edward G. Robinson as Steve Wilson, courageous editor of The Illustrated Press, with Claire Trevor as his star reporter, Lorelei Kilbourne. Later, radio actors Edward Pawley and Fran Carlon took over the roles.

...the Shadow knows!™ "

J. Scott Smart as **The Fat Man**

The FBI in Peace and War *(1944-1958)* dramatized actual case histories from the files of the Federal Bureau of Investigation; **The Adventures of Bulldog Drummond** *(1941-1954)* featured a sophisticated English detective, who "came out of the fog and into his American adventures" as quite a foil to the hard-boiled detectives so popular at the time. The man even had a chauffeur. But Drummond, played by Ned Wever among others, was tough enough to beat the bad guys; **Boston Blackie** *(1944-1950)* with actor Richard Kollmar, was a former criminal turned crime fighter who was tough and trouble proned but with softer edges than really tough guys; **Casey, Crime Photographer** *(1945-1950)* starred Staats Cotsworth as crime-solving Casey, Jan Miner as newspaper reporter Ann Williams, and John Gibson as Ethelbert, the bartender at the Blue Note Bar, Casey's and Ann's favorite after-work hours hangout; and **The Mollé Mystery Theater** *(1943-1954)* sponsored by Mollé Shaving Cream, presented a different mystery story each week on **The Mysterious Traveler** *(1943-1952)*, with Maurice Tarplin as the narrator/traveler, presented spine-tingling tales of murder and suspense–the stuff of nightmares.

Escape *(1947-1954)* opened with its memorable promise, "Tired of the every day world? Want to get away from it all? We offer you....escape!" And they always delivered. **Famous Jury Trials** *(1936-1949)* presented dramatizations of actual courtroom cases; **Mr. District Attorney** *(1939-1954)* with Jay Jostyn as the crime-solving D. A., Len Doyle as his assistant, Harrington, and Vicki Vola as his secretary, Miss Miller; always punished the bad guys "to the limit of the law;" Arch Oboler's spooky **Lights Out** *(1935-1947)* became a classic scream-and-scare anthology series; private eye **Mr. Chameleon** *(1948-1953)* with Karl Swenson as the title

Philip Clarke as **Mr. Keen, Tracer of Lost Persons**

character, was the master of many disguises, key to his crime-solving; **Mr. Keen, Tracer of Lost Persons** *(1937-1955)* starred Phil Clark, and later Arthur Hughes, the soft-spoken, "kindly investigator" who sought, and always found his quarry; **Nick Carter, Master Detective** *(1943-1955)* starred Lon Clark as the fast-living, intellectual detective, with Charlotte Manson as his sexy enumerate, Patsy Bowen; **Quiet Please** *(1947-1949)* had Ernest Chappell playing the leading role in a different drama each week and **The Saint** *(1945-1951)* presented Vincent Price in the title role of the sophisticated crime-fighter who used logic and his great charm to solve cases.

1934  **1935**  **1937**  **1939**  **1943**

Witch's Tale　　　　　　Lights Out　　　　　　Tracer of Lost Persons　　　　I love a Mystery　　　　Nick Carter-Master Detective

Jack Webb as Sergeant Joe Friday with partner Barton Yarborough of **Dragnet**

This Is Your FBI *(1945-1953)*, like the FBI In Peace and War, dramatized actual cases; **The Fat Man** *(1946-1951)* opened with unforgettable, "There he goes…across the street…into the drugstore. Steps on the scale. Height: six feet. Weight: 290 pounds. Fortune: Danger! Whooo is it? The Fat Man!" J. Scott Smart played the corpulent P. I., Brad Runyon a character created by Dashiel Hammett Ironically, Hammett, whose literary output was relatively small, probably had more heroes on radio than any other well known mystery writer; Alonzo Dean Cole's creepy **Witch's Tale** *(1934-1937)* at one time starred teen-aged actress Miriam Wolfe as the narrator/witch, Nancy, who spun a variety of weird tales of horror and the supernatural weekly; Carlton E. Morse's **I Love A Mystery** *(1939-1957)* was one of America's favorite mystery shows in the late 1930's and early 1940's, when it starred Michael Raffetto, Barton Yarborough, and Walter Paterson as P.I.s Jack Packard, Doc Long, and Reggie Yorke, owners of the A-1 Detective Agency. The show started as a daily serial, complete with cliffhanger closings, then became a half-hour program complete with each episode. But in the 1950's, it returned to its five-day-week format, this time starring Russell Thorson, Jim Boles and Tony Randall as Jack, Doc and Reggie; **Yours Truly, Johnny Dollar** *(1949-1962)* starred, over its long run, Charles Russell, Edmund O'Brien, John Lund, Bob Bailey, Bob Readick, and finally, Mandel Kramer as "the insurance investigator with the action packed expense account," **Johnny Dollar; Dragnet** *(1949-1956)* with its low-keyed, "Just give me the facts, ma'am," police work of Sergeant Joe Friday, played by actor Jack Webb, had a style unique in the annals of police procedure. It became, for a while, a national craze and remains, to this day, one of the most mimicked programs of any time–on radio, and later television and films.

1944 **1945**  **1946**  **1949**

Boston Blackie · This Is Your FBI · The Fat Man · Quiet, Please

"Calling the police! Calling the G-Men!"

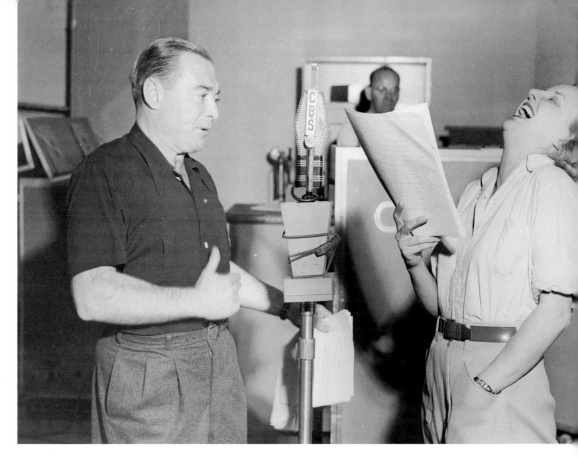

Inner Sanctum rehearsal with
Peter Lorre and Elspeth Eric

Raymond Edward Johnson, "Your Host,"
welcomes listeners to **Inner Sanctum**

Top Rated

In addition to **The Shadow**, the three most listened to, loved and remembered mystery/crime/horror shows of Radio's Golden Age were **Gangbusters**, **Inner Sanctum Mysteries**, and **Suspense**. They are among the programs that make up the radio legend, and are names familiar even to folks who never heard the originals.

Gangbusters *(1935-1957)* made its radio debut on the CBS network of stations and remained one of the most popular shows on the air until radio began to lose its audience to television. Called G-Men when it was first aired, Gangbusters was one of radio's more violent shows. Produced by Phillips H. Lord and narrated by Lord and Colonel H. Norman Schwarzkopf, the show featured crime stories, which were sometimes fact and sometimes fiction. The weekly casts included some of radio's hardest working actors, including Mercedes McCambridge, Richard Widmark, Mason Adams, Art Carney, Alice Reinheart, Robert Dryden, Santos Ortega, Bill Zuckert, Larry Haines, Ralph Bell and Elspeth Eric. Eric, who specialized in playing the show's gunmolls, was so popular she received hundreds of fan letters after every episode from inmates of various prisons around the country. Each weekly program opened with the sounds of marching feet, machine-gun fire, and a wailing siren. A voice then called out, "Calling the police! Calling the G-Men! Calling all Americans to war on the underworld," followed by the announcer's booming voice saying, "Gangbusters! With the cooperation of leading law-enforcement officials of the United States, Gangbusters presents facts in the relentless war of the police on the underworld...authentic case histories that show the never-ending activity of the police in their work of protecting our citizens."

Inner Sanctum Mysteries *(1940-1952)*, a weekly fest of horror, and/or ghosts and murder, was the brainchild of prolific radio producer-writer-director Himan Brown. Each week, "Your Host Raymond" (first played by Raymond Edward Johnson, then Paul McGrath) welcomed listeners through "the squeaking door" into the inner sanctum where murder, mystery and mayhem ruled and ghosts and goblins were commonplace. The series became a weekly "must" for millions of listeners all across the United States. As on Gangbusters, many familiar voices were heard on each episode. Among them were Mercedes McCambridge (called "the world's greatest radio actress" by no less an authority than Orson Welles), Everett Sloane, Ann Shephard (a.k.a. Scheindel Kalish), Mason Adams, Myron McCormick, Karl Swenson, and others.

Over the years, Inner Sanctum was sponsored by Carter's Little Liver Pills, Palmolive Brushless Shaving Cream, and Lipton Tea.

Suspense

She (Bette Davis) awakens–tied, in a darkened room–to the realization that the screams she had heard in the nightmare were her own. She is in the young man's room (played by Elliot Reed), and he is sitting across from her in the dark. He tells her softly that he must kill her.

One of the longest running, most critically acclaimed programs on the air, as well as one of radio's last popular mystery shows, was **Suspense** *(1942-1962)*. Calling itself "Radio's outstanding theater of thrills," this series was, indeed "well calculated to keep you in... Suspense!" Originally produced and directed by Charles Vanda, it was the talented radio director William Spier who steered the program into the national spotlight, and made it a favorite even after its radio life (on TV). Early in the series' run, Spier had the brilliant idea to cast leading Hollywood film stars in roles that they would not normally play in the movies. Such popular performers as Rita Hayworth, Betty Grable, Lucille Ball, Charles Laughton,

Olivia deHavilland, Lana Turner, Judy Garland, Robert Taylor, James Stewart, Joan Crawford, and many others, including such unlikely mystery protagonists as Jack Benny, Fibber McGee and Molly (Jim and Marian Jordan) and Mickey Rooney surprised and delighted audiences. The program's most popular script, however, was "Sorry, Wrong Number," and starred Suspense regular Agnes Moorehead, a talented character actress as well known for radio as she was for film, and later television. The script was written by Lucille Fletcher and first aired in the mid 1940's. It was repeated by popular demand many times in the years following, with Miss Moorehead always in the leading role. It had such impact that it was made into a major movie, with Barbara Stanwyck as the main character. This almost painfully suspenseful tale is about a wealthy, bed-ridden woman, with a nasty, selfish whine, who is left alone in her New York City townhouse because her husband is purportedly away and her maid has the night off. She tries to make a phone call, when she accidentally cuts into another line, and overhears two men planning the murder of an unnamed woman. While our main character, makes phone call

after phone call, trying desperately to report this future murder to anyone who will listen, she gradually comes to realize that she is the intended victim. The story ends with the high-pitched scream of the woman, still in bed and still on the telephone, covered by the sound of a passing train, as the murderer does her in. He then picks up the still-engaged phone and says, "Sorry... wrong number." The Suspense program was sponsored by Roma Wine for many years and then by Autolite Spark Plugs.

Each Monday, CBS Radio's **Gunsmoke** recreates life in the West of the 1880's through the actions of U.S. Marshall Matt Dillon. Here, at a rehearsal conference, the cast listens to the instructions from producer-director Zorman Macdonnell (far left). Fourth from left is William Conrad who stars as Matt Dillon

An Adult Western

Children had their favorite Western programs like **The Lone Ranger** and the **Roy Rogers and Gene Autry Shows**, but the adults had **Gunsmoke** *(1952-1961)*. One of the last drama series on the radio, Gunsmoke dealt with such adult themes as alcoholism, child abuse, and murder. It starred veteran radio actor William Conrad as Sheriff Matt Dillon, a no-nonsense Dodge City lawman in the late 1800's. Dillon's special friend, saloonkeeper Miss Kitty (Georgia Ellis), his deputy, Chester Proudfoot (Parley Baer), and his friend Doc Adams (Howard McNear) were an integral part of each week's drama.

CHAPTER THREE

Comedy

Bud Abbott and Lou Costello's Debate
"Who's On First"

Comedy

Abbott and Costello

Two types of comedy shows emerged during The Golden Years of Radio. They were the comedy/variety program and the situation comedy. Comedy/variety shows were similar to vaudeville shows, which the public was already familiar with when radio first began to attract their attention. A star comedian (or pair of comedians) was the central character, and musical selections (either orchestral or vocal) were the breaks between the comedy monologues and sketches. The star usually played a distinct character on the show. Ed Wynn, for example, was "a perfect fool," Jack Benny was the quintessential miser, and Fred Allen was a wise, witty, somewhat caustic observer.

The situation comedy, on the other hand, was comparable to a one-act play, each a complete story that centered on the same major character every week. For example, the wise-cracking, single teacher looking for a husband; the beautiful, loveable dim-wit, who could get a husband if she wasn't on the edge of disaster all the time; the immigrant, whose English is a mind-boggling hoot; the pretentious saloon manager, whose vocabulary is at odds with his garbled grammar, and his personality totally lovable, and so on.

Comedy/Variety

The legendary silent screen star Mary Pickford, once "America's Sweetheart," took to the airwaves on the NBC Blue network in 1934, as her film career was on the decline. Her program, **Parties at Pickfair** *(1934-1936)*, was broadcast from Pickford's legendary estate of the same name. Pickfair had become famous in the press for the fabulous Hollywood parties she, and by now ex-husband, Douglas Fairbanks, threw for the elite of Hollywood. The listening public was delighted to be weekly "guests" at Pickfair. Each week, Mary hosted a fabulous party at which celebrated film stars such as Bette Davis, William Powell, Constance and Joan Bennett acted in dramatic and comedy sketches. Bing Crosby, Russ Columbo, Gene Austin, and Gertrude Neisen provided the music. It was probably more variety than comedy, but the mood was up and happy, and there were more than a few laughs.

The same year Parties at Pickfair made its NBC debut, CBS introduced **Hollywood Hotel** *(1934-1941)*. Similar in format to Pickford's program, this show featured such regulars as newspaper gossip columnist Louella Parsons, as well as the more conventional type of performers a la motion-picture singing star Dick Powell, pop singers

Frances Langford, Frank Parker, and Anne Jamison (a.k.a. "Jinnie, the soprano"), and Ted Fio Rita and his orchestra as regulars. An impressive array of Hollywood personalities as guest stars added to the life of the show, which lasted longer than Parties at Pickfair. After creating a sensation as guests on **The Kate Smith Show**, performing their legendary "Who's On First?" baseball routine, the comedy team of Bud Abbott and Lou Costello were given a show of their own called–what else?–The **Abbott and Costello Show** *(1940-1949)*, it was an instant hit. It remains one of America's all time favorite comedy programs. The show was much like their films, with their characters firmly established in the minds of listeners. Abbott was the acid-tongued, wisecracking straight man, and Costello, was the child-like, innocent buffoon who provided most of the laughs. But the best remembered show was not a comedy at all. It was, in fact, tragic, and illustrated the immediacy of radio to give us the news. In the midst of the program, the show stopped cold, and it was announced that Lou's little son had drowned in the family pool. The show did not go on. Millions of Americans were shocked, and spent a night close to tears.

The Andrews Sisters

The **Andrews Sisters Show** (1944-1946) featured the swing-singing trio, Patty, Maxene and Laverne, who also made appearances on many other major radio shows. The sisters' show had originally been called The Andrews Sisters Eight to the Bar Ranch when it first went on the air, and co-starred Western sidekick/funny man, George "Gabby" Hayes. Shortly after its debut, the program was renamed The Andrews Sisters Show, the Western setting was abandoned, and singer Kurt Massey replaced Hayes as the girls' costar.

Bob Hope and guest, Doris Day

The **Al Pearce Show** (1933-1946) was one of radio's most successful programs for all of its thirteen years. Pearce was smart enough to play the straight man to several hilarious characters on his show, such as Mr. Kitzel (Artie Auerbach, who later joined the cast of the Jack Benny Show), Lizzie Tish (Bill Comstock), the Laughing Lady (Kitty O'Neill), Yahbut (Jennison Parker), and The Human Chatterbox (Arlene Harris). Pearce, himself, in addition to his relatively unrewarding straight-man duties, also played the amusing characters Elmer Blurt and Eb on the show. Marie Green and Her Merry Men provided musical interludes.

The **Bob Hope Show** (1934-1955) starred the quick-witted, smart-mouthed comedian Bob Hope, and featured a zany cast of regulars, including bushy-mustached comedian Jerry Colonna, the man-hungry Vera Vague (Barbara Jo Allen), and Brenda and Cobina (Elvia Allman and Blanche Stewart), L. C. Sivony (Frank Fontaine), and such musical favorites as singers Peggy Lee, Frances Langford, Marilyn Maxwell, Judy Garland, the Andrews Sisters, and Al Goodman and his orchestra. Hope reached the zenith of his radio fame with his wartime broadcasts, performed before thousands of GI's in remote regions of the world, often close to the major battle zones of World War II. His Christmas broadcasts were especially poignant due to his ability to make mothers, fathers and sweethearts at home feel close to their loved-ones overseas as they listened to Hope's broadcasts. They were grateful to Hope and his company for caring for their loved ones, and these, and his continuing shows and broadcasts to entertain the military abroad, became part of his legend.

The **Chase and Sanborn Hour With Edgar Bergen and Charlie McCarthy** (1928-1948) turned ventriloquist Edgar Bergen and his wooden-headed, top-hatted, monicled dummy, Charlie McCarthy, into two of the world's biggest stars. Could Bergen's weekly listeners see whether he was a great ventriloquist, whose lips didn't move when he spoke for Charlie? No–and they didn't care. They just loved the big guy and his fresh little sidekick. As it turned out, Bergen wasn't such a good ventriloquist, but the material, and the characters he created were prime. When The Chase and Sanborn Hour made its radio debut, film actor Don Ameche was the show's master of ceremonies, but he was soon overshadowed by Bergen and his dummies Mortimer Snerd, whose name became synonymous with country bumpkin, and Effie Klinker, a gossipy old maid. Such musical talents as Anita Gordon, the King Sisters and Dale Evans were featured on the program regularly. Two of radio's most publicized episodes of all time took place on this show. On the first, film comedian W. C. Fields

had an all-out, all-for-fun fight with Charlie, which had listeners laughing and talking about it for weeks. On the other, film Sex Queen Mae West exchanged suggestive remarks with Charlie, and audiences laughed even harder. These programs are considered two old-time radio classics.

Vaudeville and Broadway headliner, Eddie Cantor, who had been heard on the Ziegfeld Follies of the Air in the 1920's, debuted on his own **Eddie Cantor Show** in 1938. He was one of radio's brightest stars and his show remained on the air until 1949. Surrounded by talented singers such as Dinah Shore, Deanna Durbin, Bobbie Breen, Margaret Whiting, and comic regulars like The Mad Russian (Bert Gordon), with his weekly greeting, "How-do-you-do," Greek food vendor Parkyakarkis (Harry Einstein), real-life violinist Dave Rubinoff (whose speaking voice was supplied by Lionel Stander, and then Alan Reed), and Madamoiselle Fifi (Veola Vonn). Cantor remained at the top of the radio-show ratings for the program's full run.

Edgar Bergen and Charlie McCarthy

Fred Allen

Before he became a star and one of radio's greatest wits, Fred Allen was a moderately successful vaudeville performer. His low-keyed, nasal voice was unique, and made him a natural for radio because it made him so easily identifiable. But it was his droll delivery and incredible wit that made him a star. **The Fred Allen Show** *(1931-1949)* was an audience favorite largely because of its very funny sketches, mostly written by Allen himself. The most famous of the sketches was the comedian's weekly visit to Allen's Alley, home to some of the funniest characters on radio. There, Fred and his real-life wife Portland Hoffa would interview the screwy inhabitants, asking each a topical question of the day, such as, "Do you think Santa Claus will get down the chimney this year?" and "Why does the Lone Ranger wear a mask?" always with hilarious results. The denizens of the Alley were ham actor Falstaff Overture (played by Alan Reed); Jewish housewife, Pansy Nussbaum (Minerva Pious) who talked a lot about her off-mike husband Pierre; New England farmer, Titus Moody (Parker Fennelley); Irish loudmouth, Ajax Cassidy (Peter Donald), and a politician-windbag, Senator Claghorn (Kenny Delmar). Fred's character, and the superb supporting cast who played them, became as popular as Allen himself. Fred's musical guests included the Andrew Sisters, the DeMarco Sisters, and Kenny Baker among others.

Jack Benny

Fred Allen's radio rival, although their famous "feud" was strictly a publicity stunt, was the ever-popular Jack Benny. **The Jack Benny Program** *(1932-1958)* was radio's most successful comedy show. He and his long time regular cast members–Mary Livingstone (his real-life wife); his black valet, Rochester (Eddie Anderson); his announcer, Don Wilson; bandleader, Phil Harris, and tenor, Dennis Day, became as familiar to audiences as their families. Jack's stinginess; his long, pregnant pauses when asked something he didn't wish to respond to, and then his answer, "I'm thinking...I'm thinking" when pressured; the safe where he kept his money, hidden in the depths of his basement and guarded by a man who hadn't seen the light of day in years (played by comedian Mel Blanc); his exchanges with an officious department-store floorwalker, who also turned up at various other localities (Frank Nelson) and always greeted Jack with an unctuous "Yeeeees!"; his on-the-phone flirting, and then dates, with two tough, Brooklyn-accented telephone operators named Mabel and Gertrude (Bea Benaderet and Sara Berner); and other routines too numerous to mention, but equally as memorable, are still enjoyed today via cassette recordings of The Jack Benny Show. They give testimony to Benny's timeless humor. His long-time sponsors, whose products became totally identified with the comedian, were Jello puddings and Lucky Strike cigarettes.

Judy Canova

sidekick Cliff Hall and his comic, "Vas you deere, Sharlie?" and "You make me so madt!" spoken with a heavy German accents were imitated endlessly across the U. S.

Film and stage comedian Jimmy Durante's successful radio show initially co-starred funnyman Garry Moore. It was called **The Durante and Moore Show** and was retitled **The Jimmy Durante Show** *(1943-1950)*, when Moore departed to pursue a solo career. In addition to Jimmy's "inka dinka doo" musical antics and his sublimely ridiculous malapropisms, two very popular characters contributed to the success of the program–Candy Candido, who always answered Jimmy's, "How are you?" with, "I'm feeling mighty low," his voice dropping down several octaves; and Hotlips Hoolihan, played by Florence Halop, who had a heavy Brooklyn accent and was always chasing after one man or another. The two very funny actors were as essential to the show as Durante himself.

Country singer and comedienne, Judy Canova, enjoyed great success on radio with her **Judy Canova Show** *(1943-1953)*. Judy played herself, as a character that was pure country. She lived with her Aunt Aggie (Verna Felton) and maid, Geranium (Ruby Dandridge) and had weekly visits from such humorous characters as her Mexican pal Pedro (Mel Blanc); her weary neighbor Mr. Hemingway (Hans Conreid), who

Another "Jack" who enjoyed a long career as a radio comedian was Jack Pearl. Pearl's **Cresta Blanca Carnival and Lucky Strike Program** ran in succession from 1932 until 1951. Pearl's most popular radio characterization was Baron Munchhausen, his own version of the legendary untruth teller. His banter with

had too many children at home to deal with; Joe Crunchmuller (Sheldon Leonard), a New York con artist; Count Benchley Botsford (Joseph Kearns), an effete Englishman, and Mrs. Atwater (Ruth Perrott), a gushy society lady. Musical numbers sung by Judy and her many other country-artist guests were the highlights between the laughs.

An amusing musical variety-quiz show starring bandleader Kay Kyser, who had a flare for comedy, became one of radio's surprise hits in 1938 and remained on the air for eleven years. Called **Kay Kyser's Kollege of Musical Knowledge**, Kay called on members of the studio audience to answer musical questions, but they mainly served as springboards for the music of Kyser, and the comedy bits performed by orchestra members like Ish Kabibble (Merwyn Bogue). Ginny Simms and Harry Babbitt provided the vocals and became very popular with the audience at home.

Jimmy Durante

Kay Kyser's Kollege of Musical Knowledge

Fanny Brice as **Baby Snooks**

Major Bowes and His Original Amateur Hour *(1934-1952)* was a weekly talent contest that gave amateur performers a chance to be heard in their quest for fame and fortune. The show was hosted by "Major" Edward Bowes, who would open each week's program saying, "The weekly wheel of fortune…around and around she goes, and where she stops, nobody knows!" He would then introduce, and briefly interview, a wide variety of amateur performers, from whistlers and spoon players, to vocalists and comedians, who vied for the audience's applause, which determined the show's winner. Several winning contestants, such as Frank Sinatra got his first national exposure on this program, their earliest steps to superstardom. More often than not, however, the contestants' show-business aspirations ended with one appearance on The Original Amateur Hour.

ShowBoat *(1932-1941)* was a variety show featuring a Mississippi River steamboat as its setting. When it first went on the air, actor Charles Winninger was its host, Captain Henry, and such talented performers as Hattie McDaniel (Mammy), Molasses and January ("Pick" Malone and "Pat" Padgett) rounded out the cast of characters. Singers Lanny Ross, Rosaline Green, Nadine Connor, the Westerners, and orchestra leaders Donald Voorhees and Al Goodman performed regularly. The show was sponsored for many years by Maxwell House Coffee.

Situation Comedies

In 1942, NBC presented a weekly situation comedy that was based on Ann Nichols long-running Broadway comedy, **Abie's Irish Rose** *(1942-1944)*. The half-hour episodes involved a Jewish boy, Abie Levy, (played by Richard Coogan and Bud Collyer, among others), and his young Irish-American bride, Rosemary Murphy (Betty Winkler, Mercedes McCambridge and Julie Stevens during various periods) and the difficulties they encounter with their Jewish and Irish families and friends who do not exactly approve of this mixed marriage. The couple's fathers, Solomon Levy (played at times by Charlie Cantor, Alan Reed and Alfred White) and Patrick Murphy (Walter Kinsella), constantly argue on the show, but basically like each other. The comic sensations of the series, however, were their neighbors, the Cohens, played by longtime stars of the Yiddish stage, Menasha Skulnick and Anna Appel. The Cohen's spoke with heavy Yiddish accents, and their amusing exchanges became the highlight of each episode. Various groups, protesting the stereotyping of Irish and Jewish people, eventually managed to have the show cancelled. NBC removed it from their roster while it was still at the top of the ratings.

When bandleader Ozzie Nelson first decided to create a weekly comedy series based on his own family life, co-starring his wife Harriet, everyone thought the program was doomed to fail. But **The Adventures of Ozzie and Harriet** *(1946-1949/NBC; 1949-1954/ABC)* surprised everyone with its cozy, domestic success. Ozzie, as chief writer, set the everyday family tone and low-key style. The characters of sons David and Ricky were always part of the typical American family adventures, although they did not play themselves until 1949. The all-American family (we thought back then) began broadcasting their popular show, complete with sons Ricky and David, on television in 1952 where it enjoyed even greater success.

Like Abie's Irish Rose, another successful Broadway play, **What A Life**, also found its way to radio. Retitled **The Aldrich Family** *(1939-1953)*, the show's major character was trouble-prone teenager Henry Aldrich, an American youth, with all of the problems a young man trying to succeed in school and entering the world of dating, usually has. The show opened with Henry's mother calling, "Henry…Henry Aldrich!" To which Henry would answer, "Coming, Mother!" in the cracking, adolescent voice that would become so associated with Ezra Stone, who played Henry for most of the weekly series run. It also became one of radio's best-remembered introductions. Adding to the show's humor and domestic atmosphere were the warm performances of House Jameson and Katherine Raht, most memorable of the actors who played Henry's parents, and Jackie Kelk, who played Henry's best friend Homer for most of the show's run.

Before turning to Radio, comedienne Fanny Brice was a major stage star headlining in vaudeville, the Ziegfeld Follies, and nightclubs. As a guest on radio's **Good News**, Fannie performed a sketch featuring one of her stage characters, Baby Snooks, a hilariously bratty child, which she had created for the Follies. The response to Brice's performance was so strong and positive she was offered a comedy series of her own. Week after week, Brice, as **Baby Snooks** *(1944-1951)*, together with her long-suffering Daddy (first played by film actor Frank Morgan, then for most of the series' run by Hanley Stafford), her somewhat dithery mother (Arlene Harris) and her baby brother, Robespierre (acted by baby-voice specialist, Lenore Ledoux) made listeners laugh their way through one episode after another on one of America's favorite situation comedies.

Comic strip characters were naturals for radio, so it was no surprise when the celebrated **Blondie** *(1939-1950)* arrived on CBS radio. Chic Young's comic strip of the same name was read by millions in the Sunday papers as well as the dailies, and had inspired several movies, starring Penny Singleton and Arthur Lake as Blondie and husband Dagwood Bumstead, before hitting the airwaves. The same actors played the pretty blonde, hat-buying wife, and the bumbling husband who ate foot-high sandwiches in the dead of night on the radio show. Listeners, therefore, were already familiar with the voices, and had a good idea of what the characters looked like. It was the kind of familiarity that bred success.

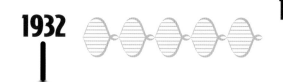

1932

1934

1935

George Burns and **Gracie Allen**

One of radio's best situation

comedies was "The Burns

and Allen Show"

One of radio's best situation comedies was **The Burns and Allen Show** *(1935-1950)*. The husband and wife team of George Burns and Gracie Allen were already big stars in vaudeville and films, before they turned to radio. George was the somewhat gruff, but always patient husband to Gracie's addle-pated, dithery wife, whose rambling brain circuitry could, in fact, try the patience of a saint. But George always seemed as amused by her as we were. He was the best straight man in the business. Listeners loved the contrast, and the team went on to weekly television success after the Golden Age of Radio came to an end. But before that, in 1940, Gracie decided to run for the office of President of the United States on the "Surprise Ticket." It was a publicity stunt, but Gracie treated it like the real thing, and made countless guest appearances on every other major radio show to promote her "campaign." Burns and Allen's popularity soared even higher.

1939  **1942**  **1944**

The Aldrich Family   Abie's Irish Rose   Baby Snooks

A Date with Judy

A Date With Judy *(1941-1950)* featured a teenager named Judy Foster as its central character. The weekly comic situations dealt with all of the problems, joys and complications of adolescence. Judy was played by several actresses over the years, including Dellie Ellis, Louise Erickson and Ann Gillis. Her younger brother, Randolph, a prominent character on the show, was played by Dix Davis, her dad by Stanley Farrar, Joseph Kearns, John Brown over the years, and her mom variously by Lois Corbett, Bea Benaderet, and Myra Marsh. Jack Benny's singing tenor, Dennis Day had a radio show of his own, **A Day In The Life of Dennis Day** *(1946-1951)*. Day, as talented a comedian as he was a singer, played a somewhat naive young bachelor, a character he had developed on the Jack Benny Show.

One of radio audiences' favorite and best-remembered comedy series was **Duffy's Tavern** *(1941-1951)*. For all of its years on the air, the show was consistently voted one of radio's best in Radio Guide and Radio Mirror magazines listener polls. The show starred Ed Gardner as Archie, manager of a tavern in lower Manhattan. Characters such as the dim-witted Finnegan (Charlie Cantor), and Miss Duffy, the tavern owner's daughter (once played by Shirley Booth), Eddie, the bartender (Eddie Green), and Clancy the cop (Alan Reed) all kept the show at the top of the ratings. Duffy, the owner, was never heard on the show, and, in truth, did not exist, but he seemed a regular character because Archie, the manager, was always speaking to him on the phone, a tribute to Gardner's acting. Practically every major star in Hollywood and Broadway eventually turned up as customers at Duffy's Tavern at one time or another. In 1945, Paramount Pictures produced a star-studded film set in Duffy's Tavern, with many of the radio cast in attendance, including Ed (Archie) Gardner, who was given star billing. Every major star, on contract to Paramount at the time, appeared as patrons.

Although it is difficult to place them in any single category, two of radio's most popular shows, **Easy Aces** *(1931-1949)* and **Ethel and Albert** *(1944-1950)*, both about the "little things in life" that exist between a husband and wife, certainly depended on situations and were unquestionably comedies. The difference between these and other situation comedies is that most of the action on these shows was revealed through conversation. We couple these programs together because they had so much in common. While not commanding the biggest audiences, both did have the longest-lived, most loyal listeners and were what we today call "cult" shows. Both starred the people who created and wrote them–Goodman Ace (who played himself on Easy Aces) and Peg Lynch (the Ethel of Ethel

and Albert). On Easy Aces, Goodman had the perfect foil in his real life-wife, Jane, who played a scatterbrained, illogical, but very funny, lady. If anyone could make us see him roll his eyes by voice only, it was Goodman. Ethel's mate, Albert, played by actor Alan Bunce, was her sometimes exasperated, but always loving, husband. This show could have been a model for TV's hit-show Mad About You. Both of these shows kept their loyal audiences for their entire time on radio, and tapes of old broadcasts, plus recent new Ethel and Albert episodes (they're middle-aged now) prove these shows to be as fresh and original as when they were first aired.

Fibber McGee and Molly

Unquestionably, the most successful and beloved of all radio's situation comedies were **Fibber McGee and Molly** *(1935-1956)*. Former vaudeville comedians Jim and Marian Jordan, a husband-and-wife team, first created their Fibber McGee and Molly characters for a show called Smackouts, and also made successful appearances on **Don McNeills' Breakfast Club**, before being given a series of their own. Fibber McGee was a braggety, know-it-all but lovable windbag, and his wife, Molly, was the perfect forbearing, kind wife, who knew Fibber's shortcomings, but loved him anyway. The couple, as everyone across the nation knew throughout the 1930's and 1940's, lived at 79 Wistful Vista, in a typical, American small town. The zany

The contents of Fibber McGee's closet are finally revealed. Here NBC's sound effects man, Howard Tollefson has carefully arranged Fibber's collection and awaits his cue to start the bedlam heard when the closet is opened on NBC's "Fibber McGee and Molly" program heard on Tuesday nights at 9:30.

Jim and Marian Jordan play the title roles of **Fibber McGee and Molly**

assortment of characters that appeared on the show regularly were no small reason for the program's enormous success. In addition to Molly, the multi-talented Marian Jordan also played such characters as a little neighborhood girl named Teeny, who asked Fibber some question on each episode, and then countered each of his answers with, "Why?" Her own observations and replies were punctuated with the phrase, "I betcha." Marion also played Mrs. Wearybottom, Lady Vere-de-vere, and Geraldine. Other popular characters were the McGee's black maid, Beulah, played by white actor Marlin Hurt (so popular that he was given a spin-off series of his own, Beulah), Throckmorton P. Gildersleeve, the McGee's bloated next-door neighbor, played by Hal Peery (who was also given a spin-off, the phenomenally successful show, The Great Gildersleeve), Mayor LaTrivia, played by Gale Gordon, Doc Gamble, played by Arthur Q. Bryant, and the rich Mrs. Uppington, played by Isabel Randolph. Fibber McGee and Molly's long-time sponsor was Johnson's Wax Company and Harlow Wilcox, who appeared as himself on the program, was also the announcer.

The Great Gildersleeve

When Throckmorton P. Gildersleeve was given a show of his own, **The Great Gildersleeve** *(1941-1956)*, he needed a job, and became a small-town water commissioner with a nephew, Leroy (Walter Tetley) and niece Majorie (Lurene Tuttle, then Louise Erickson) to raise. His Black housekeeper, Birdie, (Lillian Randolph) helped him keep things in as much order as possible, but Gildersleeve's bragging and general ability to make more of things than they were always got him into trouble. A bachelor, Gildersleeve's engagement, first to Southern Belle, Lilah Ransom (Shirley Mitchell) and then Eve Goodwin (played first by Bea Benaderet, then Cathy Lewis) were fraught with trouble but always funny affairs. Gildersleeve's friends, Floyd the barber (Arthur Q. Bryant) Peevey, the mealy-mouthed druggist (Richard LeGrand, then by Forrest Lewis) and Oliver Honeywell (Hans Conreid) could always be depended upon to keep the laughs coming.

Nobody expected **Life With Luigi** (1948-1953) to succeed, but film character actor J. Carrol Naish, himself an Irish American, played recent Italian immigrant, Luigi Basco, with such a convincing aura of gentle sweetness, the audience was captivated, and remained so for years. One of the show's funniest characters was Luigi's boss, Pasqual (Alan Reed), who had brought Luigi to America hoping to marry him to Pasqual's obese, unattractive daughter, Rosa (Jody Gilbert). Luigi's fellow immigrants at the night school where they studied English were Horowitz (Joe Forte), Schultz (Hans Conreid) and Peterson (Ken Peters). The show's theme music, "Oh, Marie," and Luigi's rendition of "America, I Love You," which he sang at the end of each show, became indelibly identified with this show.

No show was more listened to in rural America than **Lum and Abner** *(1935-1953)*-and a large part of America was rural during its run. On the air for over twenty-two years (the first few years on local radio), it was the situation comedy second only to Fibber McGee and Molly in popularity. Lum (played by Chester Lauck) and Abner (Norris Goff) exemplified the small town, rural Americans so many people strongly identified with, and their homespun, gentle humor struck a familiar but somehow surprisingly funny note in people, keeping them tuned in week after week. Partners Lum and Abner owned the Jot 'Em Down Store and Library, a kind of jumble shop, selling everything from lye soap to stoves to used books–a little bit of this, a little bit of that–in the fictitious town of Pine Ridge, Arkansas. By 1936, the show had become so popular, the town of Waters, Arkansas, officially changed its name to Pine Ridge. Frequent customers hanging around Lum and Abner's potbelly stove were such country characters as Grandpappy Peabody, Snake Hogan, and Cedric We Hunt (all played by Lauk), and Dick Huddleston, the town postmaster, Doc Miller, and Squire Skimp (played by Goff). Others heard on the show from time to time were Zasu Pitts, Cliff Arquette, Edna Best, Cornelius Peeples, and Andy Devine.

GILDY'S JOY -"The Great Gildersleeve" in a pose he enjoys-surrounded by young lovelies. The girls showering their attention on the water commissioner of mythical Summerfield are (left to right) Alice Drake, Julie Bennett and Barbara Fuller.

Like A Date with Judy, **Meet Corliss Archer** *(1943-1954)* revolved around a typical American teen, with a penchant for getting into trouble, always with comic results. Janet Waldo, Priscilla Lyon, and Lugene Sanders played the title role over the years, and Fred Shields, Bob Bailey, Irene Tedrow and Helen Mack played her parents at various times. Corliss' boyfriend, Dexter Franklin, one of the most popular characters on the program, was played by Sam Edwards, then David Hughes. Fuffy, Corliss' best friend, was played by Barbara Whiting.

In the early 1950's, many radio situation comedy series became popular television series as well. **Meet Millie** *(1951-1954)* was one such program. The radio version starred film star Audrey Totter as the single working girl, Millie, with Bea Benaderet as her widowed mother who was always concerned that her daughter would never marry.

Another successful radio-to-television crossover was Lucille Ball's **My Favorite Husband** *(1948-1951)*. It was the forerunner of the later, beyond successful, I Love Lucy television show. Both shows followed a similar format, and both programs were written by Bob Carroll, Jr. and Madelyn Pugh. On the radio, actor Richard Denning played Ball's husband, but in the transition to television, Lucy's real-life husband, Desi Arnaz, became her small-screen spouse, and the rest was history.

Yet another hit show that made its way to television was **My Friend Irma** *(1947-1954)*. The half-hour situation comedy starred Marie Wilson as Irma Peterson, a dumb but gorgeous blonde, who worked as a file clerk in a big city office. Irma's brainy roommate, Jane Stacy, played by veteran radio actress Cathy Lewis, narrated each week's episode. A wild assortment of characters was featured on the show: Irma's con-artist boyfriend, Al, played by John Brown, her always flustered boss, Mr. Clyde, played by Alan Reed, her Irish landlady, played by Gloria Gordon, and fellow boarder in Irma and Jane's rooming house, Professor Kropotkin, played by Hans Conried. The show remained at the top of the ratings each year it was on the air, and even spawned a successful film starring Marie Wilson as Irma and Diana Lynn as Jane.

Blue-collar workers had a champion in Chester A. Riley, the central character on **The Life of Riley** *(1944-1951)*. Played by screen actor William Bendix, Riley was a factory worker who came home to a loyal, long-suffering loving wife named Peg (played over time by Grace Coppin, Georgia Backus, and Paula Winslow), and two teenaged children, Babs (variously played by Peggy Conklin, Sharon Douglas, and Barbara Eiler) and Junior (Jack Grimes, Scotty Beckett, Conrad Binyon, and Tommy Cook). Riley's unsophisticated innocence, his tendency to screw up, then observing the mess with, "What a revoltin' develpment this is!" kept the laugh meter high. His amusing friends, such as Digger O'Dell, the friendly undertaker (John Brown), neighbors Gillis and his wife, Honeybee (Brown and Gloria Blondell), and his Uncle Barker (Hans Conried) were no small part of the show's success. Riley made a smooth transition to television, with Jackie Gleason as the title character for a short period of time. Then Bendix again took over the role.

Our Miss Brooks *(1948-1957)* also made a seamless transition from radio to television in the mid 1950's, largely due to its star, Eve Arden, who had already made a big splash in films. From the program's initial airing, Connie Brooks was everyone's favorite high school English teacher, due mainly to Arden's brilliant comedic acting. On radio, as on screen, she was the wise-cracker with the heart of gold, and just as importantly, she had perfect timing. The supporting characters on Our Miss Brooks always got their share of the laughs. They were: Connie's ever-flustered boss, Madison High School Principal Osgood Conklin (played by Gale Gordon); her elderly landlady, Mrs. Davis, (Jane Morgan), her favorite student, Walter Denton (Richard Crenna), and her heartthrob, science teacher, Mr. Boynton, played by yet-to-be movie star, Jeff Chandler.

The low-keyed **Vic and Sade** *(1932-1944)* straddled the fence between amusing soap opera and situation comedy, but either way, its loyal listeners loved it. Vic and Sade Gook were a typical American couple who just happened to say funny things and know some very eccentric people. Art Van Harvey played Vic and Bernadine Flynn, his wife, Sade, for the entire time the show was aired. The Gooks lived "in a little house halfway up the next block" with their son, Rush (played by Billy Idelson, Johnny Coons, and Sid Koss over the years), and their Uncle Fletcher (Clarence Hartzell). Many zany characters, who were talked about, but never heard, seemed as tangible, and as funny as Vic and Sade themselves perhaps because of their unforgettable names: Lottie Sterienzi (Vic's secretary), Jake Gumpox (the garbage man), Smelly Clark (often-quoted pal), Ruthie Stembottom (Sade's friend who went to wash-rag sales at Yamelton's Department Store), Ishigan Fishigan of Sisigan, Michigan (who always called Vic long distance), and the twins Robert and Slobbert Hink (who sent Vic and Sade postcards from unusual places).

Before there was "I Love Lucy," Lucille Ball starred in **My Favorite Husband** on CBS. Actor Richard Denning played Ball's husband

CHAPTER FOUR

Music Programs

Music Programs

Music has always been, and still is, a natural for radio and there was no shortage of great offerings. But two of those programs, you might say, ruled, and their two stars, Bing Crosby and Kate Smith, became the giants of the music world, owing much of their success to radio.

Crooner Bing Crosby had a show of his own on radio as early as 1931, but became a major star when he took over **The Kraft Music Hall** in 1933 from the show's original star, Al Jolson. In time, the program's name was changed to **The Bing Crosby Show**, and remained on the air until 1956. It always began with Bing singing his theme song, "Where the Blue of the Night Meets the Gold of the Day," which he first performed in the film, The King of Jazz, in 1930. His weekly guests included such masters of music as the Boswell Sisters, the Andrews Sisters, the Mills Brothers and Judy Garland. Bing presented listeners with the very best in American popular music, and remained on the air well after most big-name singers had abandoned radio for television. His announcer Ken Niles, and his resident orchestra led by John Scott Trotter, and his backup singers, The Modernaires, were parts of the program's straightforward, no-nonsense, strictly musical makeup. Not that the show was humorless. Bing was great at between-song banter and guest appearances by his pal and film partner, Bob Hope, periodically lightened things up. But music was the main event.

From the time **The Kate Smith Show** (1931-1949) debuted, its full-throated, rich-voiced hostess became inextricably identified with both radio and America. No less than Time Magazine called Kate "the first lady of radio." It was perhaps her rendition of "God Bless America," which she made nationally famous, that caused the public to think of her as a talisman for the American way, synonymous in those days with the free, democratic, right way. Indeed, Kate lived up to her image by raising six hundred million dollars in war bonds during World War II, via arduous personal appearances around her beloved country. But it was her music listeners appreciated most, and she sent many songs soaring to national fame, including "When The Moon Comes Over The Mountain," which became as closely identified with her as "God Bless America." At the height of her radio career, Smith, with the help of her long-time partner/manager and sometimes co-host, Ted Collins, was responsible for the radio debuts of such superstars as film actress Greta Garbo, comedian Bert Lahr, actor John Barrymore, comedians Abbott and Costello, and Henny Youngman. In 1938, Kate also became the hostess of **Kate Smith Speaks**, a talk show that remained on the air until 1951. She also made a successful transition to TV in the 1950's. Her image and her sound remained firmly fixed in people's minds long after she was able to perform regularly. In the most cynical of times and by the most cynical of people, she was still the good and true American.

One of radio's earliest musical successes was **The American Album of Familiar Music** (1931-1951). An hour-long offering, heard over the NBC network of stations, The American Album featured such acclaimed classical and semi-classical singers as tenors Frank Munn and Donald Dane, sopranos Evelyn McGregor, Jean Dickenson (called "the nightingale of the airwaves"), and Eleanor Lennox, as well as the Buckingham Choir, pianists Arden and Arden, and Gustave Haenschen's Orchestra. The formidable voice and diction-perfect speech of announcer/host Andre Baruch was just right for the high-toned musical program.

The Bell Telephone Hour (1940-1958) was another classical and semi-classical music program that had a long run on radio. Donald Voorhees led the show's orchestra, which backed such well-known singers as film star-baritone Nelson Eddy, contralto Marian Anderson, sopranos Grace Moore Bidu Sayao, Lily Pons, and Helen Traubel, tenor James Melton, and Ken Christie's Mixed Chorus. At one time, the show was hosted by "the voice" of Alexander Graham Bell, as performed by radio actor Raymond Edward Johnson.

The Ben Bernie Show (1933-1943), hosted by the orchestra leader of the same name, featured an impressive array of musical talent–vocalists Buddy Clark, Dinah Shore, "Little" Jackie Heller, Mary Small, Jane Pickens, "Scrappy" Lambert, and many others. The show's closing became almost as famous as the program itself, with Bernie saying, "And now the time has come to lend an ear. Au revoir. Pleasant dreams. Think of us when requesting your themes."

The Carnation Contented Hour (1931-1951), sponsored by Carnation Evaporated Milk, featured the Percy Faith, Josef Pasternack and Frank Black Orchestras over the years as well as popular singers Buddy Clark, Jo Stafford, soprano Gladys Swarthout, and many other well known singers of the day. The program's announcers, Vincent Fletcher, Bret Morrison, and Jimmy Wallington successively hosted this program of semi-classical and musical-comedy selections.

A musical program that featured a generous dose of comedy, along with a proliferation of music was the wonderfully titled **Chamber Music Society of Lower Basin Street** (1940-1952). This program highlighted the musical talents of Dinah Shore, Jane Pickens, and Lena Horne, and the comic routines of such funny fellows as Zero Mostel. Mainly a jazz and swing program, the show attracted considerable attention and had a big weekly audience.

For fifteen minutes a day, **The Chesterfield Supper Club** (1944-1950), sponsored by Chesterfield cigarettes, starred Jo Stafford, Perry Como, Bill Lawrence, Peggy Lee, Frankie Laine, the Pied Pipers, Fred Waring and His Pennsylvanians Orchestra. It also featured the orchestras of Glenn Miller, Paul Weston, Tex Benake and Sammy Kaye, at various times during its run. **Club Fifteen** (1948-1953) followed the same format, with similar high-rated results, and starred, Jo Stafford, Margaret Whiting, the Andrews Sisters, the Modernaires, Evelyn Knight, Giselle MacKenzie, Dick Haymes, Bob Crosby's Bobcats and other musical favorites over the years.

Fred Waring and His Pennsylvanians (1931-1957) were on and off the air for almost thirty years in various show formats. The orchestra and chorus leader's regulars included the Lane Sisters, Honey and the Bees, Stella and the Fellers, tenor Gordon Goodman, soprano Jane Wilson, guitarist Les Paul, and singer-comedienne Kay Thompson, during the years Fred's shows were being broadcast regularly.

The grandpappy of all music/variety shows, **The Grand Ole Opry**, was heard on radio as early as 1925, and can still be heard, as a syndicated show, on local radio stations throughout the nation. Considered to be the best country music show ever, The Grand Ole Opry, was first broadcast from a small studio in a local radio station, and then, as its fame grew, from its very own theater, The Grand Ole Opry House. Both studio and Opry were–and are– in Nashville, Tennessee, the home of country and western music. During its years on the air, The Grand Ole Opry show has boasted appearances by every major star in the country and Western music scene. These artists include Red Foley, who hosted the show for many years, Gene Autry, Roy Acuff, Hank Williams, Patsy Cline, Loretta Lynn, Ernest Tubbs, Eddie Arnold, the Cumberland Mountain Boys, Willie Nelson, and many others. Comedy is not the most important thing here, but such country clowns as "Cousin" Minnie Pearl, "Grandpa" Jones, and Rod Brasfield provided funny interludes.

A Sunday morning ritual for a considerably large audience was **The Hartz Mountain Canaries** (1938-1945). The incredible stars were, in fact, canaries, which sang along with the Hartz Mountain Orchestra as they played such favorites as "Ah Sweet Mystery of Life" and "I'm Only A Bird in A Gilded Cage." Jess Kirkpatrtick was the show's host.

Phil Spitalny led his celebrated All Girl Orchestra on one of radio's all time favorites, **Hour of Charm** (1934-1948). One of the show's most popular attractions was Evelyn and Her Magic Violin (Evelyn Kaye Klein). Also popular were vocalists "Maxene," "Jeanie," and Hollace Shaw (called "Vivien" on the show), and Katherine Smith and Her Coronet. Arlene Francis, Rosaline Green, and Barbara Lee hosted the show, at different times.

The Lanny Ross Show originally called **Mardi Gras/The Packard Show** (1928-1952), starred singer Lanny Ross. Ross was known as "the Troubadour of the Moon," because he introduced "Blue Moon," which became a hit, and his theme song. His crooning was romantic, and his handsome face seen on hundreds of radio-fan-magazine covers certainly didn't harm his popularity. Regulars on Ross' program included singers Evelyn Knight and Louise Carlyle, the Buddy Weed Trio, and Will Lustrin's Orchestra.

Your Hit Parade (1935-1956) not only went from radio to television without hitches in the 50's, at one point it was broadcast on both media. But either way, the format was always the same. Each week, usually on Saturday night, regular cast members would sing the top ten top songs of the week, as compiled by recording-industry surveys. Over the years, regular singers on the show included Frank Sinatra, Joan Edwards, Georgia Gibbs, Bea Wain, Lawrence Tibbett, Eileen Wilson, Dinah Shore, Andy Russell, Doris Day, Lanny Ross, Marie Green, Beryl Davis, and many others. Your Hit Parade's various orchestras were led by Al Goodman, Freddie Rich, Lennie Hayton, Johnny Green, Richard Himber, Axel Stordahl, and Orrin Tucker (the last featuring singer "Wee" Bonnie Baker as his vocalist).

CHAPTER FIVE

Popular Children's Programming

A fiery horse
with the speed of light,

Popular Children's Programming

Miriam Wolfe, expert actress in the role of fairy tale witches, is joined at the microphone by starlets Joan Lazer and Judith Lockser to enact the program inaugurating the **Let's Pretend** series' 18th year of broadcast over the Columbia network

Children's Series

There was no shortage of children's programs during Radio's Golden Age, and they ran the gamut from narrated (unacted) story-telling and song shows, with such performers as **The Singing Lady** *(1931-1945)*, starring Ireene Wicker, and **Uncle Don** *(1929-1949)*, starring Don Carney and Howard Rice), to adventure and crime-fighting series. But there was one show that stood alone as a children's dramatic anthology, **Let's Pretend**, so special that even during its run records were made of some of the episodes, so that children could hear them over and over again at will.

The creative genius behind CBS' **Let's Pretend** *(1931-1954)* was a lady named Nila Mack. She not only directed the series, but also adapted most of the fairy tales dramatized on the program, and even wrote some original fantasies for it. Heard on Saturday morning for most of its years on the air, Let's Pretend featured a cast of regular players that included "Uncle Bill" Adams, who hosted the show, and narrated parts of the fairy tales; young actors Sybil Trent and Patricia Ryan, who played most of the heroines; Miriam Wolfe, who played witches and wicked queens, as well as kind spirits and mothers; Albert Aley, Bill Lipton, Jack Grimes, and Larry Robinson, who played leading men; and Arthur Anderson, Gwen Davies, Michael O'Day, Bob Readick, Donald

Hughes, and others, who filled the various character roles. Most of these actors began their Let's Pretend appearances when they were children, and grew into young adulthood right in front of the microphone. Over the years, kids were treated to such classic fairy tales as Cinderella, Jack and the Beanstalk, Sleeping Beauty, The Night before Christmas, Snow White and Rose Red, as well as Miss Mack's original stories. The show's familiar theme song, performed by Sybil Trent and Gwen Davies at the beginning of each show, was sung to the tune of Komzacks' Fairy Tales. It served as both the opening of the show and the sponsor's first commercial message–and the kids at home often sang along:

Cream of wheat is so good to eat
Yes, we have it every day.
We sing this song, it will make us strong
And it makes us shout Hooray!

It's good for growing babies,
And grownups, too, to eat,
For all the families breakfast
You can't beat Cream of Wheat!

Children's Adventure Serials

Each weekday, Monday through Friday, from five to six P.M., at least one radio in the house was given over to the children of the house. It was after school, and probably right in the middle of playtime, but nothing could empty a street filled with the busiest of kids than a cliff-hanging radio adventure. Many of the shows were based on children's favorite comic book and comic-strip stories, so they knew what the heroes and heroines looked like. And it wasn't just each episode, with its promise of new peril for their hero, that made them come back for more. There were also those wonderful premiums--the decoding rings and badges, games and club booklets, etc.–which you could get if you sent in the sponsor's box top or label and "one thin dime." Among the kids favorite serials were: **The Adventures of Red Ryder** *(1942-1949)*, **Straight Arrow** *(1948-1951)*, **Bobby Benson's Adventures (Bobby Benson and the B-Bar Riders)** *(1932-1936 & 1949-1955)* all Westerns; **Buck Rogers in the 25th Century** *(1932-1947)* science fiction; **The Adventures of Dick Tracy** *(1935-1948)* police adventure; **Don Winslow of the Navy** *(1937-1943)* military adventure; **Hop Harrigan** *(1942-1950)* daredevil aviation; **Jungle Jim** *(1935-1952)* and **Tarzan** *(1932-1953)*, adventures in the wild; **Popeye, the Sailor** *(1935-1938)*, humor, and **The Sea Hound** *(1942-1951)*, adventures on the seven seas.

The most popular children's daytime serials, were **Jack Armstrong, the All American Boy, Little Orphan Annie, Terry and the Pirates, Superman,** and **Sky King**. Only two early-evening adventure shows, written primarily for children, could compete–the legendary **Lone Ranger** and **The Green Hornet**.

When children heard the opening of the **Jack Armstrong** *(1933-1950)* program, which began: "Jack Armstrong… Jack Armstrong… Jack Armstrong, the All American Boy!" and then heard a quartet sing:

Wave the flag for Hudson high, boys,
Show them how we stand!
Ever shall our team be champions,
Known throughout the land!

Followed by the sponsor's:

Have you tried Wheaties?
They're whole wheat with all of the bran.
Won't you try Wheaties?
The best breakfast food in the land!

they knew they were in for fifteen minutes of high adventure and thrills. Jack, a heroic young high school student (played over the years by St. John Tyrell, Jim Ameche, Charles Flynn, Rye Billsbury, and Dick York), together with his friends, could always be counted upon to chase down criminals, spies (during World War II), and various other nasty villains, and bring them to justice. Jack's earliest adventures were set at the World's Fair of 1933, in Chicago.

A child who was very adept at battling evil-doers each afternoon was **Little Orphan Annie** *(1935-1943)*. Annie (played by young actress Shirley Bell), her Daddy Warbucks (played by many actors), and dog Sandy fought many a dangerous battle together, with most of the danger hanging over poor Annie's head. But she was a feisty little girl who never wavered in the face of danger if the cause was just. Annie's sponsor, Ovaltine, and the show's opening theme song:

Who's that little chatterbox?
The one with all those curly locks?
Who can she be?
It's Little Orphan Annie!
She and Sandy make a pair,
They never seem to have a care.
Cute little she,
Little Orphan Annie!

were as familiar to listeners as the Little Orphan Annie herself.

Captain Midnight *(1939-1949)* was a heroic character created especially for radio. The Captain (played by Ed Prentiss, Bill Bouchey and Paul Barnes over the years) was a pilot who flew his single-engine plane all over the world seeking adventure. Youngsters especially appreciated his heroics during the World War II years, when he sounded the call to arms and fought the evil Axis forces. Kids sent for Captain Midnight decoding badges and rings, and war charts and guide books, and believed they were aiding the war effort by using them.

Taken from Milton Caniff's successful comic strip, radio's **Terry and the Pirates** *(1937-1948)*, captivated kids from the moment Terry Lee and his pals took to the airwaves. Terry was played in succession by Jackie Kelk, Cliff Carpenter, and Owen Jordan; his friend Patrick Ryan by Bud Collyer among others, Flip Corkin by Ted de Corsia, and a girl named Burma by Frances Chaney. But the most vivid character was Terry's chief nemesis, the evil, gorgeous, sexy, frightening, never-to-be-forgotten Dragon Lady (played by Agnes Moorehead, Adelaide Klein, and Marion Sweet over the show's run). This Oriental dish of villainies plotted evil in the several exotic Far Eastern settings where the show took place.

"Faster than a speeding bullet…more powerful than a locomotive…able to leap tall buildings in a single bound. Look! Up in the sky! It's a bird! It's a plane! It's Superman!" So started each episode of **The Adventures of Superman** *(1938-1951)*, as kids eagerly awaited the daily adventures of one of their favorite heroes. They loved him as much on radio as they did in the comics and apparently couldn't get enough of the caped crusader. Clayton "Bud" Collyer brought superman–and Clark Kent– to life on radio. He was often joined in his crime-fighting activities by fellow superhero, Batman, played by Stacy Harris, and Batman's ward, Robin, played by Ronald Liss.

Pilots were extremely hot heroes during the 1930's and 40's, at first a response to World War aviation victories, then as a desire to use them personally in peacetime. One post-war fictional pilot, who captured children's imaginations with his fifteen-minute, weekday, radio adventures, was **Sky King** *(1946-1954)*. Sky King (played by Jack Lester, Earl Nightingale and Roy Engel) owned a ranch so vast, he needed his airplane to keep an eye on his property. However, more often than not, he used his plane to track down various criminals, with the help of his two young wards, Penny (Beryl Vaughn) and Chipper (Jack Bivens), and his ranch foreman, played by Cliff Soubier. The team never failed to apprehend a wicked rustler or an outlaw.

Bud Collyer who starred as **Superman**

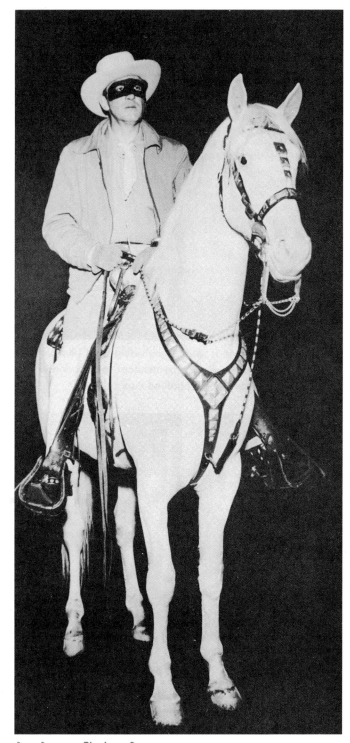

Brace Beemer as **The Lone Ranger**

Children's Evening Series

The creators of **The Lone Ranger** *(1933-1955)* were George W. Trendle and Fran Striker, and their opening is perhaps one of radio's (and later television's) most remembered. It began with the music of Rossini's "William Tell Overture" and the sound of galloping hoofbeats, then the Ranger shouting, "Hi-yo, Silver, away!" Then the show's announcer (for many years Fred Foy) would set the premise:

A fiery horse with the speed of light, a cloud of dust and a hearty hi-yo, Silver!
The Lone Ranger!
With his faithful Indian companion, Tonto, the daring and resourceful masked rider of the plains led the fight for law and order in the early Western United States.
Nowhere in the pages of history can one find a greater champion of justice.
Return with us now to those thrilling days of yesteryear.
From out of the past comes the thundering hoofbeats of the great horse, Silver.
The Lone Ranger rides again!

The Lone Ranger voice most people remember was Brace Beemer's, who played the role for the longest period of time. John Todd played his faithful Indian companion, Tonto, very active in crime-fighting activities. Our masked stranger did have a past–known only to listeners and Tonto. He'd been a Texas Ranger, surname Reid, who had suffered a vicious attack by outlaws. Tonto found him and nursed him back to health. Upon his recovery, Reed dedicated his life to battling evildoers, a vow shared by Tonto. He always wore a mask in public–to make him anonymous to strangers–both those he helped (who initially distrusted him, and from whom he wanted no thanks or entanglements), and those he fought (villains who found the mask fearsome). He always used silver bullets in his revolvers, and left immediately upon solving all problems. As he rode away, someone would invariably ask, "Who was that masked man?" The reply was always, "You don't know? Why that's the Lone Ranger!" It's hard to overestimate the success of The Lone Ranger. His clean living habits and moral convictions made him a perfect role model for youngsters, and millions of parents all across the country eagerly encouraged their children to listen to the program. Some of them enjoyed the show as much as their children did. The half-hour series originated from WJZ radio studios in Detroit, and was heard two or three evenings a week. Unlike most of the children's daytime programs, The Lone Ranger's adventures were complete with each episode––a series, not a serial.

The Green Hornet *(1938-1953)* was closely related to The Lone Ranger–a grand-nephew actually. Developed by Fran Striker and George W. Trendle, The Green Hornet was in response to his original concept of a masked man–this time a modern–day masked man who answered to the name of Britt Reid when he wasn't in Hornet costume. Over the years the character was played by Al Hodge, Donovan Faust, Bob Hall, and Jack McCarthy. Like his ancestor, Reid wore a mask, plus a whole Green Hornet disguise, to hide his identity and anonymously fight "the biggest game of all, public enemies who try to destroy America." There were other parallels between the Ranger and the Hornet. The Lone Ranger had his faithful Tonto, and the Green Hornet had his loyal Japanese--and then when World War II broke out, Fillipino--manservant Kato as his assistant in chasing criminals. The Ranger depended upon his "great white horse, Silver" for speedy transportation, the Hornet used his sleek, black automobile, "Black Beauty," which sounded like a buzzing hornet as it carried him from one crime solving mission to another. The two shows also shared the same group of actors for their supporting casts. For Striker and Trendle, classical music was an apparently important part of their creations. For The Green Hornet, the theme music was "The Flight of the Bumble Bee." This early-evening, half-hour series also originated from Detroit's WJZ, and aired once a week.

The Roy Rogers Show *(1944-1955)* starred filmdom's "King of the Cowboys," Roy, himself, his wife Dale Evans, and character actors George "Gabby" Hayes, "Fuzzy" Knight, Forrest Lewis, and Bob Nolan. The weekly, half-hour series combined suspense-filled tales–lots of fighting the bad guys Western-style–and music, also Western style. Roy's theme song, "Happy Trails," welcomed millions of youngsters to the adventures of Roy, Trigger and the gang, and the music of Roy, Dale and the Riders of the Purple Sage.

Melody Ranch *(1940-1956)* starred the movies' "Singing Cowboy," Gene Autry. The program also contained a weekly adventure yarn, which blended with Gene's wonderful cowboy songs to make for great kids' listening. The half-hour series was heard either on Sunday afternoons or evenings, depending on the season. Gene's radio sidekicks were Pat Buttram and Jim Boles. His familiar theme song, to which millions of kids at home sang along, was "Back In the Saddle Again."

Daytime Programming For The Ladies

Daytime Programming for the Ladies

Breakfast Shows

David Gothard and Julie Stevens had leading roles in CBS' **The Romance of Helen Trent**

During the morning and early afternoon hours, radio was the territory of the millions of wives and mothers who remained at home to do household chores and take care of pre-school children. After making breakfast for work-bound husbands and school-bound kids, they could enjoy a second cup of morning coffee with Don McNeill, and his interesting guests, at his famous **Breakfast Club** (1933-1968), or lose themselves in a song, a story, and light-hearted chatter as they listened to **Arthur Godfrey Time** (1945-1956). Or they might join sophisticated married couples like **Ed and Pegeen Fitzgerald** (1940-1952), **Tex and Jinx Falkenburg McCrary** (1946-1959), or **Dorothy and Dick** (Dorothy Kilgallen and Richard Kollmar 1946-1953) at their breakfast tables, where they talked about the fabulous places they'd been the night before, told all of the latest New York and Hollywood celebrity gossip, and tuned listeners in to all the latest fads of the day.

Daytime Serials

After these early morning shows, women all across America tuned in to the trials and tribulations of ordinary, and some extraordinary women. These women were involved in the everyday problems of life. Well, maybe "everyday problems" was an understatement, and housewives were thankful their problems were, for the most part, not quite so dramatic. But whatever their own domestic complications were, five days a week, for fifteen minutes a day, Monday through Friday, these serials (later called "soap operas," because so many of them were sponsored by soap companies) ruled the daytime airwaves. Two afternoon dramas claimed to be "the first soap opera on the air"–Himan Brown's Marie, **The Little French Princess** (1930), about a French royal who immigrates to the U.S. and finds herself leading a very ordinary life, and **Clara, Lu, and Em** (1930-1945), a serial about three gossips who knew everyone and everything that was happening in their hometown. Both of these shows were totally overshadowed by the subsequent, long running (some ran for as many as thirty years) drama serials that followed. Clara, Lu and Em did have a healthy fifteen-year go at it, but never reached the top of the heap. Here are those that did.

Oxydol's own **Ma Perkins** (1933-1960) was one of the last and longest running soap operas, heard on radio. The serial, about an elderly Ma (played for the series' entire run by Virginia Payne), her two daughters, Evie (Rita Ascot, among others) and Fay (Laurette Fillbrandt, and others), and Ma's partner at The Rushville Center Lumber Yard, Shuffle Shober (Charles Egleston).

The Romance of Helen Trent (1933-1960), also one of the last and most popular serials on radio had one of the most famous openings: "The Romance of Helen Trent... who sets out to prove to herself what so many women long to prove, that because a woman is thirty-five or more...that romance can live in life at thirty-five or after." Helen was played by many actresses over the years, probably most notably by Julie Stevens, and had more romances than anyone else on radio.

Two of daytime drama's unforgettable openings were heard on **Our Gal Sunday** (1936-1959) and **When A Girl Marries** (1939-1959). Both shows' openings clearly state the premises of the programs. Our Gal Sunday began by asking the question, "Can a girl from a mining town out West find happiness as the wife of a wealthy and titled Englishman?" Not easily, much to the appreciation of the listeners. When A Girl Marries' opening stated that it was "...a tender, human story of married life... dedicated to everyone who has ever been in love," and we understood that the course of true love never did run smoothly. Sunday was played for many years by Vivian Smolen, and "the girl who married," Joan Davis, was played by Mary Jane Higby.

Other popular daytime serials heard during Radio's Golden Age were: **John's Other Wife** *(1936-1942)*, about a young married couple and his "other wife," who was his loyal, loving (but not in that way) secretary, with Joseph Curtin, among others, playing John; and **Stella Dallas** *(1937-1955)*, played for many years by actress Anne Elstner, which was a continuation on the air of the true-to-life story of mother love and sacrifice. Stella saw her own beloved daughter, Laurel, ("Lolly, baby" played by Vivian Smolen) marry into wealth and society and, realizing the differences in their tastes and worlds, went out of Laurel's life forever. Based on the film Stella Dallas, "forever" was the operative word in terms of life with Laurel. But on radio, Stella and "Lolly" were into each other's pockets every day of the week; and **Life Can Be Beautiful** *(1938-1954)* was affectionately known as Elsie Beebee (L.C.B.B) to actors who enjoyed working on the show. It was centered around the lives of the kindly Jewish owner of "The Second Hand Bookshop," Papa David Solomon, (played by Ralph Locke), and his young wards, Chichi, (Alice Reinheart) and Steve Hamilton (Earl Larrimore, and then John Holbrook.) Their problems were central to the show–maybe Chichi found out the guy who liked her was married, and Steve discovered he was inadvertently being sucked into the underworld. But no matter how tough the situation, Papa David's advice saved the day.

Two young women, trying to break into show business, were the heroines in **The Story of Myrt and Marge** *(1931-1942)*, written by and starring Myrtle Vail as Mert, and Vail's daughter, Donna Damerel, playing her friend, Marge, also an aspiring actress.

Another behind-the-scenes, show-business story that was enjoyed by millions of women each day was Mary Noble, **Backstage Wife** *(1937-1959)*. Mary (played by actress Vivian Fridell, among others) was an ordinary, unassuming young woman who was married to matinee idol, actor Larry Noble (James Meighan, and a myriad of others). Well, you can imagine the unexpected pitfalls of such an unlikely union like the exciting women after your husband, who you fear are more attractive than you, the difference in their worlds, the problems that popped up when other folks had problems.

Later on, in the fabled history of radio, humorists **Bob and Ray** *(1946-1960)*, a.k.a. Bob Elliott and Raymond Goulding, improvised a brilliant spoof of the show, Mary Backstage, Noble Wife, which only helped immortalize the serial.

Two serials that featured female characters in hospital settings, a natural location for soap-opera action on both radio and television, were: Joyce Jordan, **Girl Intern** *(1938-1956)*, a young woman doctor, (most notably played by Betty Winkler, and then Elspeth Eric), and **The Woman In White** *(1938-1948)*. The latter centered around a nurse, Karen Adams Harding (originally played by Luise Barkley), who had a penchant for trouble and a talent for becoming involved with the wrong men.

No soap opera heroine was more long-suffering or resourceful, however, than Portia Manning (played by Lucille Wall), a lawyer who tried to find time to deal with both a successful career, during which she battled local corruption, and her numerous domestic problems, including several husbands, on **Portia Faces Life** *(1940-1952)*. Well, maybe Ellen Brown (played by Florence Freeman) came close on **Young Widder (Widow) Brown** *(1938-1956)*, about a young woman determined to make a new life for herself after the death of her young husband. The opening of Portia Faces Life, which stated that it was "a story that reflected the courage, spirit and integrity of American women everywhere," could have served as an introduction for both of these shows.

Every woman who listened to daytime serials believed, as stated in the introduction to a favorite daytime drama, that they had "**A Right to Happiness**" *(1939-1960)*. But the serial's heroine, Carolyn Kramer Nelson (played by Claudia Morgan and then Eloise Kummer) seemed to have more troubles than joy, including the deaths of several husbands and several problem children to raise. But it was a character named Rose Kransky (played by Ruth Bailey); a down-to-earth girl who was introduced on **The Guiding Light**, who became the audience's favorite character.

Men were the title characters on four of radio's most popular serials. **Lorenzo Jones** *(1937-1955)* was played by Karl Swenson. A mechanic by

vocation, he was a dreamer and inventor by calling. He hoped one day to invent something that would make his fortune, and was always lovingly supported in his efforts by his wife Belle (played by Betty Garde, then Lucille Wall) even though they were likely to end with funny consequences.

Just Plain Bill *(1935-1955)*, known as barber Bill Davidson on the serial, and played by Arthur Hughes, was a kind-hearted, elderly gentleman, to whom the folks in his hometown, Hartville, turned to for advice and guidance. Bill never let them down. Described in the show's introduction as "a man who might be your next door neighbor," the audience profoundly hoped so.

Pepper Young's Family *(1933-1959)* was the continuing story of a young man, Pepper Young, just starting out in life, and trying to find his way in a difficult world–first through work, then marriage, children, etc. For many, years, Mason Adams played Pepper, with Betty Wragge as his sister Peggy. **Young Doctor Malone** *(1939-1960)* was about Jerry Malone (most memorably played by Alan Bunce, and then Sandy Becker) and the problems he faced as a young physician and new husband.

The Longest Running Drama on the Air–and Still Going

One daytime drama serial, which has certainly stood the test of time, made its radio debut in 1937 and can still be seen on television today. We're talking about **The Guiding Light**, which left radio in 1956. (It had already started broadcasting on TV even while on radio.) In its earliest days, the show told the story of a small town minister, Dr. John Rutledge (played by Arthur Peterson), who was constantly attempting to solve the problems of members of his congregation and/or his young daughter, Mary (Mercedes McCambridge). It was Rutledge and his church that provided the show's "guiding light". But eventually the series took off in different directions and the Rutledges disappeared. The Bauer family became the series' central characters--and their troubles were legion. Today, many characters share the spotlight, but some of the Bauers are still there and in full peril.

David Gothard, Patricia Dunlap, Ken Griffin, Vivian Fridell and Alice Patton of **Backstage Wife** heard over the NBC-Red network every weekday at 4:00 p.m.

Hugh Studebaker, left, played the role of kindly minister Dr. Charles Matthews, in a scene in CBS' daytime drama, **The Guiding Light** with Willard Waterman and Betty Lou Gaerson, who portrayed ex-convict Ray Brandon and his friend Charlotte Wilson.

Continuing Nighttime Troubles

Two soap operas were popular evening attractions on radio (one for over twenty years) –**Those We Love** and **One Man's Family**.

According to Radio Guide Magazine, **Those We Love** *(1938-1945)* was one of the top-ten shows in America during 1939 and 1940. It documented the many trials of the Marshall family, who lived in a small town in Connecticut. Film star Francis X. Bushman, among others, played lawyer John Marshall, the widower-patriarch of the Marshall clan, who was trying to keep his twins Kathy (Nan Grey) and Kit (Richard Cromwell, then Bill Henry) on the road to a good life. After an unfortunate romance, Kathy discovered the romantic Dr. Leslie Foster, played by Donald Woods, whose sexy voice made a big impact on the ladies. But most of the audience also knew what film actors Woods and Grey looked like, handsome and gorgeous, and often

shown on the covers of radio fan magazines. Their looks were a big part of their popularity, and their romance was fodder for national conversation. Aunt Emily Mayfield, also an audience favorite, was played by veteran Hollywood character actress, Alma Kruger, later well known as Nurse Molly Bird in the **Dr. Kildare** *(1950-1951)* radio show, and the popular MGM film series, based on the same character.

No nighttime serial enjoyed the popularity and longevity of the legendary **One Man's Family** *(1933-1959)*. In 1939 and 1940, its ratings placed it among the top five shows in the nation, beating many of the giants of prime-time radio. It sustained an audience of 15 million for years. The story, centering on the Barbour family, was unfolded in "chapters" and "books" and by the time the series left the air, 134 books had been aired. The drama was penned by one of radio's finest writers, Carlton E. Morse, and centered on the Barbour family of San Francisco. Henry Barbour, played by J. Anthony Smythe for the entire run of the program, was a crusty, sensible, conservative man who worked as a

stockbroker. His wife Fanny, played for many years by Minetta Ellen, was loyal, loving, and gentle. Their children included eldest son Paul (Michael Raffetto), a former World War I pilot; Hazel (Bernice Berwin); the twins Claudia (Kathleen Wilson) and Clifford (Barton Yarborough) and the "baby" of the family, Jack (Page Gilman). Listeners literally grew up with the Barbour children as they fell in love, married, were widowed and had children of their own. These children eventually became major characters on the series. There was also always a special Christmas show, with the Barbours gathered together, trimming the tree, opening presents, and for many families at home, it became a ritual to listen in. For them, Christmas would not have been Christmas without the Barbours.

The cast of
One Man's Family

Dramas and Anthology Shows

Adaptations of classic novels, plays, and films, as well as dramas written especially for radio, were very well listened to during this "golden" period. Incidents from history and current news stories were also dramatized on such programs as **Cavalcade of America** *(1935-1953)* and **March of Time** *(1931-1945)* two very successful programs, especially popular during World War II. **Dr. Christian** *(1937-1954)*, which starred film actor Gene Hersholt as a kindly, small-town doctor, with actress Rosemary DeCamp as his nurse, Judy, and **Mayor of the Town** *(1942-1949)* with character actors Lionel Barrymore, as a small-town mayor, and Agnes Moorehead, as his housekeeper, Marilly, both had the coziness and good will audiences loved when well presented. **The Theater Guild on the Air** *(1945-1954)*, a full hour dramatic anthology series, was a weekly program sponsored by U. S. Steel. It presented adaptations of famous plays that starred well-known actors of the theater and motion pictures. Fletcher Markle's **Studio One** *(1947-1948)* and **Ford Theater** *(1948-1949)* presented hour-long adaptations of books, films, and plays. Shortly after World War II, CBS offered the public a weekly drama series, which employed the realistic, on-the-spot, news-report format that had become familiar, via live broadcasts from battlefields, during the war. Such historical events as the landing of the Pilgrim's on Plymouth Rock, President Abraham Lincoln's assassination, and The signing of the Magna Carta were dramatized on this program called, **You Are There** *(1947-1950)*.

Top Rated Anthologies

Of all the great story-telling shows, the most famous were **The Mercury Theater of the Air, Grand Central Station, First Nighter** and the **Lux Radio Theater.**

Fresh from his triumphs on the New York stage, a young actor-director in his early twenties named Orson Welles took himself and his Mercury Theater repertory company of stage actors to the CBS microphones as he launched his **Mercury Theater on the Air** *(1937-1941)*. After one year, Campbell Soup took over as sponsor, and the weekly show became **The Campbell Theater**. Welles hosted, wrote, and usually starred in one- hour radio versions of such classics as "Treasure Island", "Les Miserables," "Dracula," and an innovative adaptation of H. G. Well's science fiction novel "The War of the Worlds" that made entertainment history. Using a "live," news style, Welles scared many U. S. citizens into believing Martians were actually invading the country. The broadcast was front-page news around the world the following day and Welles became an international celebrity. Among the many talented actors who were regulars on The Mercury Theater were Everett Sloane, Agnes Moorehead, George Coulouris, Kenny Delmar, Ray Collins, and Martin Gable.

Grand Central Station *(1937-1953)* presented original half-hour radio plays that were always connected, in some way, to New York City's celebrated train station. The show's opening is one of the most memorable ever-heard on radio:

> *"As a bullet seeks its target, shining rails in every part of our nation are aimed at Grand Central Station, the heart of the country's greatest city. Drawn by the magnetic force, the fantastic metropolis, day and night, great trains rush toward the Hudson River, sweep down its Eastern bank for 140 miles, flash briefly past the long red rows of tenement houses south of 125th Street, dive with a roar into the 2 1/2 mile tunnel, which burrows beneath the glitter and swank of Park Avenue and then…GRAND CENTRAL STATION… crossroads of a million private lives!"*

It was generally one of those million private lives that provided the weekly drama.

Each week, on **First Nighter** *(1930-1953)*, the show's host, Mr. First Nighter (for a time, Brett Morrison) would ask listeners to join him as he attended "another new play" at the fictitious Little Theater off Times Square in New York City. (Actually the show originated from a radio studio in Chicago, and then Los Angeles). There they would be treated to a half-hour drama, starring Barbara Luddy and Les Tremayne, or later Olan Soule as the leading male. The actors remained with the show for most of its years on the air. The plays ran from comedy to melodrama, to just plain drama, and Luddy was often named "Favorite Actress" in polls conducted by several fan magazines during the show's peak years in the 1940's and early 1950's.

For more than twenty years, every Monday evening was "Lux night" on radio. At nine p.m., millions of listeners eagerly tuned in to hear one-hour adaptations of famous movies, on their favorite dramatic show, **Lux Radio Theater** *(1934-1955)*. Sometimes they heard popular film stars recreate roles that they played in a movie, or sometimes there would be interesting star replacements, some famous actor in a role he or she might never play on screen. Adaptations of such classic films as "The Thin Man," "It Happened One Night," "It's A Wonderful Life," "The Wizard of Oz", "My Man Godfrey", "Great Expectations", "Dark Victory," and many others helped make Lux Radio Theater the public's favorite drama series. Guest stars like Bette Davis, Clark Gable, Claudette Colbert, Humphrey Bogart, Judy Garland, Lana Turner, Rita Hayworth, Betty Grable, James Stewart, were just a few of the many Hollywood stars who helped keep it in that top spot. And those stars looked forward to appearing before the Lux Theater microphones. Epic film director Cecil B. DeMille was the program's host until 1945, when disputes with the newly formed actor's union made him decide to leave the show. Director William Keighley took over DeMille's hosting chores that same year, and remained with the show until shortly before it departed the airwaves in 1955.

Dr. Christian

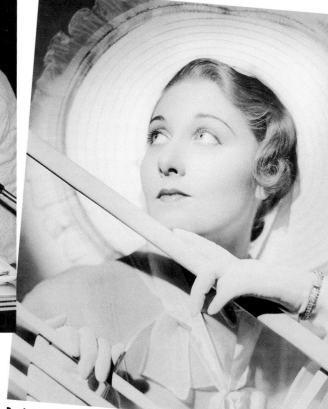

Backstage Wife with Vivian Fridell as Mary Noble

The Romance of Helen Trent with Ed Latimer, Mary Jane Higby and David Gothard

Just Plain Bill with Arthur Hughs and Ruth Russell

Carlton E. Morse stacks the volumes of "One Man's Family" scripts with the help of Mary Lou Harrington, who played Joan

Pepper Young's Family
(left to right) Jack Roseleigh, Marion Barney, Betty Wragge, and Curtis Arnall

CHAPTER SEVEN

Panel, Quiz, And Talk Shows

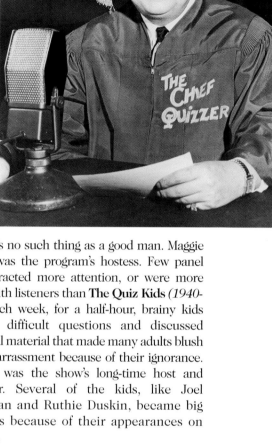

Joe Kelly on **The Quiz Kids**
(1940-1941)

Panel, Quiz, and Talk Shows

The numerous talk, panel and quiz shows which currently occupy the television airwaves, all had their origins on radio. **America's Town Meeting of the Air** *(1935-1956)*, moderated by George V. Denney, was one of the first regular political-discussion programs heard on radio. **Author Meets Critic** *(1946-1951)* was a weekly discussion program on which listeners could hear their favorite authors or some newcomers discuss their latest projects. **Information, Please** *(1938-1952)* featured a distinguished panel of intellectuals, including John Kiernan and Franklin P. Adams, who responded to Clifton Fadiman's complex questions and discussed numerous topics of general interest to the public. **Meet the Press** *(1947-1956)* was originally a Mutual show and can still be heard to this day on the NBC television network. **Can You Top This** *(1940-1954)* and **It Pays To Be Ignorant** *(1942-1951)* were two comedy panel shows that remained among America's favorite programs for all their years on the air. On Can You Top This comedians "Senator" Ed Ford, Harry Hershfield and Joe Laurie, Jr. competed to gain the highest score on an audience laugh meter as they told

jokes on a similar subject as those sent in by contestants at home. The idea was not only to beat each other, but the contestant as well. Peter Donald read the home contestant's jokes very well, and the laugh meter was in constant motion. Ward Wildon was the show's host.

It Pays to Be Ignorant featured a dim-witted panel of performers (Lulu McConnell, George Shelton, and Harry McNaughton) who were asked to answer questions like, "Who is buried in Grant's tomb?" which they never seemed to get right. An always-exasperated host, comedian Tom Howard, hosted the show. Leave It **To The Girls** *(1945-1949)* was a panel show on which guests such as Arlene Francis, Robin Chandler, Florence Pritchett, and Eloise McElhone were asked to respond to questions concerning members of the opposite sex. The question might be: How do you keep a good man? The answer might

be: There's no such thing as a good man. Maggie McNellis was the program's hostess. Few panel shows attracted more attention, or were more popular with listeners than **The Quiz Kids** *(1940-1941)*. Each week, for a half-hour, brainy kids answered difficult questions and discussed intellectual material that made many adults blush with embarrassment because of their ignorance. Joe Kelly was the show's long-time host and moderator. Several of the kids, like Joel Kupperman and Ruthie Duskin, became big celebrities because of their appearances on the show.

Newspaper columnists Walter Winchell, Louella Parsons, and Jimmy Fidler had regular celebrity news programs on the air throughout the 1930's and 40's. While Parsons and Fidler concentrated on Hollywood star and studio gossip, Winchell's programs dealt with more general celebrity items, including the comings and goings of political figures and well known criminals, as well as personalities in the entertainment world. Winchell's oft-quoted program opening was, "Good evening, Mr. and Mrs. America, and all the ships at sea. Let's go to press!"

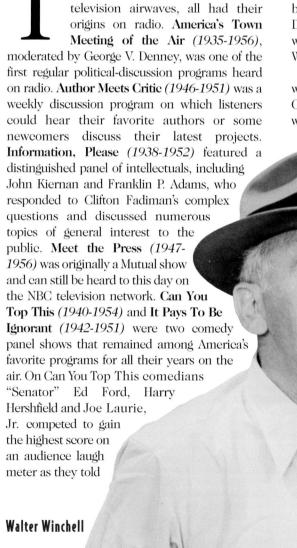

Walter Winchell

No radio talk-show hostess had more devoted fans than **Mary Margaret McBride** *(1934-1954)*. Although she never married or had children of her own, Mary had a comfortable, at-ease quality that made listeners feel as if she were a mother or daughter or some member of their own family. She first attracted attention when she was hired to be one of the "Martha Deanes," a stock name used by WOR, New York, for the female celebrity interviewer on **The Martha Dean Show**. (Obviously, there was no Martha Dean.) But Mary was so distinctive, people demanded to know who she really was, and the Mary Margaret McBride show was the result. McBride answered letters from fans asking for advice about everything from how to deal with a death in the family to how to manage the family budget. She also was very successful at getting celebrities, such as General Omar Bradley (during World War II), and aviatrix Amelia Earhart, to freely talk about their personal fears and hopes for the future.

Popular quiz shows that were heard during radio's peak years were **Ask-it Basket** *(1938-1941)*, on which four contestants could win as much as $25 for correctly answering a series of questions; **Break the Bank** *(1945-1955)*, which enjoyed a long run on radio and offered one of the highest cash prizes on the air, as much as $23,000. John Reed King hosted the show for many years; **Double or Nothing** *(1940-1953)*, on which contestants answered a series of questions and, with each correct answer, doubled their winnings; **Dr. I. Q.** *(1939-1950)* starred Dr. I. Q., called "the mental banker," was the title given to someone smart enough to be him. Lew Valentine, Jimmy McClain, and then Stanley Vainrib (all Dr. I.Q.s) answered questions asked by audience members seated all over the studio, which led to the catch phrase, "I have a lady in the balcony, Doctor." It became an oft-quoted gag throughout the U. S.; Ralph Edwards was the host of one of radio's most successful quiz shows, **Truth or Consequences** *(1940-1956)* on which a contestant, unable to answer a question, had to perform an amusing consequence, such as sliding through a hoop on a greasy floor, walking and singing like a chicken, or telling the worst joke they had ever heard. **Twenty Questions** *(1946-1954)* was an audience-participation quiz show. Listeners submitted twenty questions on a particular subject that members on a panel tried to answer. If the panel failed to answer all twenty questions, the listener who submitted the questions was awarded $75. Bill Slater, and then Jay Jackson, hosted this popular program.

A contestant, unable to answer a question on
Truth or Consequences
(1940-1956)

Sound Effects

It Pays To Be Ignorant
Tom Howard, George Shelton, Lulu McConnell, and Harry McLaughton

Mary Margaret McBride

Can You Top This?

CAN YOU TOP THIS?

Information Please

CHAPTER EIGHT

Radio News Brings World War II Home

Tokyo Rose

Radio News Brings World War II Home

Franklin Delano Roosevelt

Before World War II began, the news was usually presented in five minute reports read by local announcers in the early morning, at noon, and in the evening hours. Live news coverage of such important happenings as presidential addresses and ceremonies were only rarely heard. Inventor Lee De Forest reportedly read the first radio news item on the air in 1916, when he predicted that Charles Evans Hughes would be the next president of the United States (It didn't happen). By the time the U.S. entered World War II in 1941, the public's demand for war news encouraged the major networks to form national news departments and broadcast journalism began. Edward R. Murrow's live reports of the Battle of Britain in 1940 had already brought the devastating bombing of England by Nazi airplanes vividly alive to millions of Americans–personalizing the war and fanning the flames that eventually led to this country's entry into the war. Everybody in America could later tell you exactly where they were when they heard the news that the Japanese had bombed Pearl Harbor, Hawaii on December 7, 1941. They could also tell you where they were when President Franklin Delano

Roosevelt's declared war on Japan and Germany in his famous "day, which will live in infamy" speech. Roosevelt's voice was already familiar to listeners because of his popular Fireside Chats broadcasted regularly from the White House during the Great Depression. His articulate speech and cultured, distinctive voice proved perfect for radio, as did the voices of news commentators Elmer Davis, H. V. Kaltenborn, Lowell Thomas, Quincy Howe, and Gabriel Heatter, who kept Americans informed about the significance of the complicated political events that were unfolding daily, both at home and abroad, as the war raged on. The names and voices of on-the-scene war correspondents such as Walter Conkrite, Winston Burdette, Larry Lesueur, Eric Sevareid, William L. Shirer, Richard C. Hottelet, and Howard K. Smith, also became familiar as Americans listened to news broadcasts and reports from the front. When World War II finally ended in 1945, the entire nation celebrated after they heard about the victory on their radios. By then, "the news" had become a permanent on-air presence, as well as a significant part of people's lives.

During World War II radio protagonists

"Axis Sally" (Mildred Gillars) and "Tokyo Rose" (Iva Ikuki Toguri D'Aquino) used radio to try to convince GIs to surrender to German and Japanese forces. Few soldiers listened to what these ladies had to say, but they certainly enjoyed hearing the girls' sexy voices, and the recorded swing music from home that they played on their programs.

46

Edward R. Murrow

Command Performances

On the home front, dramatic broadcasts of plays with patriotic themes, such as Norman Corwin's acclaimed verse oratorio "On A Note of Triumph," which was heard on CBS's **Columbia Workshop** program *(1936-1957)*, effectively encouraged Americans to support the war effort.

American soldiers, sailors, and marines stationed far away from home, looked forward to listening to **Command Performance** broadcasts *(1941-1949)* produced by the Armed Forces Network. These shows offered servicemen temporary relief from the rigors of wartime activities. Command Performance was a

Left to Right: **Bing Crosby, Dinah Shore, Frank Sinatra** and **Judy Garland,** Command Performance

transcribed (recorded) program that starred some of Hollywood's and Broadway's most celebrated performers. These stars offered their services free of charge in order to help boost GI morale. They sang, acted in sketches, and sent personal greetings from the folks at home to individual servicemen who eagerly awaited each broadcast. Over the seven years it was on the air, Command Performance featured such famous performers as Bette Davis, Betty Grable, Lana Turner, singer Ginny Simms, the Andrews Sisters, Ethel Merman, Carmen Miranda, Johnny Mercer, and many others. One of the most popular Command Performance programs aired was a full-hour musical spoof of the Dick Tracy comic strip. It was called Dick Tracy in B Flat. The show starred such well known performers as the Andrews Sisters, Judy Garland, Dinah Shore, Frank Morgan, Jimmy Durante, Cass Daley, Jerry Colonna, Frank Sinatra, and the two men who were heard on more Command Performance broadcasts than any other entertainer, Bing Crosby, who played Dick Tracy, and Bob Hope, who was a humorously villainous Flattop.

Clark Gable and **Bette Davis,** Command Performance

Humphrey Bogart and **Lauren Bacall,** Command Performance, 1945

The Enola Gay takes off on its historic flight
Colonel Paul Tibbets waves goodbye just before taking off to drop the atomic bomb on Hiroshima

Walter Winchell

Pearl Harbor
Pearl Harbor, December 7, 1941. The Battleship U.S.S Arizona (right) sunk by Japanese attack planes entombing 1,102 Navy men.

Yalta
FDR with Winston Churchill and Joseph Stalin

CHAPTER NINE

Several Unforgettable Radio Moments

Several Unforgettable Radio Moments

Several memorable moments occurred on radio that left indelible impressions on the people who heard them. They have become part of our American folklore mainly by word of mouth. For those who have heard them, who could ever forget…

War of the Worlds

…Orson Welles unforgettable production of H. G. Wells' "War of the Worlds" on his Mercury Theater of the Air program. It was Halloween Eve in 1938 and unsuspecting listeners tuned in to hear what they thought was going to be a radio adaptation of a great work of literature. They were shocked when they heard a broadcast that used the on-the-air, live news report style that had become so familiar to them because of Edward R. Murrow's Battle of Britain broadcasts. Welles had adapted the science fiction novel "War of the Worlds", using the same immediate style as a newscast. Millions of listeners believed that what they were hearing was an actual invasion of Earth by aliens from the planet Mars. As preposterous as this may seem, one must remember that this type of dramatic presentation had never been heard before, and people had no way of knowing that what they were hearing was fiction and not fact. The story was a front-page item in newspapers all over the world on Halloween Day.

Orson Welles presents a radio interpretation of H.G. Wells' *War of the Worlds* as part of his Mercury Theatre of the Air on CBS radio. (October 30, 1938)

The Hindenburg

…The disastrous explosion of the German blimp, The Hindenberg, was described by newscaster Herb Morrison, who had been assigned to cover the huge craft's historic landing in New Jersey after its maiden voyage across the Atlantic Ocean. When the huge aircraft exploded as it was docking (some suspect it was pre-war anti-Nazi sabotage), Morrison's emotions and horror became apparent as his words "Oh the humanity" aired to the radio audience as he watched many people die and the aircraft burn and fall to the ground.

HISTORIC CATASTROPHE – The Hindenburg, one of Germany's luxury zeppelins, unexpectedly crashed while landing in New Jersey after a 1937 Atlantic trip.

Uncle Don

...The most famous radio faux pas... By Uncle Don, that probably never happened! Popular children's show host, Uncle Don (Don Carney and Howard Rice) was reported to have said, "Well, I guess that will hold the little bastards for a while," at the close of one of his shows, not realizing he was still on the air. The broadcast supposedly shocked the nation and had thousands of children asking what a "bastard" was. The incident became one of radio's most publicized events and hundreds of people claimed to have actually heard the broadcast. The story, however, was apparently the invention of a Baltimore, Maryland disc jockey who had told the story in order to fill airtime. The Uncle Don program was never even heard in Maryland!

Edgar Bergen and Charlie McCarthy

...Film comedian W. C. Field's live, on-the-air fight with Edgar Bergen's dummy, Charlie McCarthy, became a momentous, memorable event when the obviously inebriated Fields tore the dummy apart and threw pieces of it into the gasping studio audience.

Fiorella H. LaGuardia

...The sound of New York City's lisping mayor, Fiorello LaGuardia, reading the Sunday comics to New York's children during a 1940's newspaper strike. "Well, children," the mayor would say, "Let's see what Little Orphan Annie is doing today," and then proceed to act out all the parts in whatever comic strip he was reading.

Fiorella H. LaGuardia Speaks for Liberty

From left to right: **Edgar Bergen**, **Charlie McCarthy**, and **W.C. Fields**

John Raley in When a Girl Marries

Mary Jane Higby plays Joan Davis in When a Girl Marries

...The Sunday morning broadcast of the Hartz Mountain Canaries program when the birds stopped singing. Each week, hundreds of canaries chirped along as a studio orchestra played such semi-classical musical selections as "She's Only a Bird in a Gilded Cage" and "Ah Sweet Mystery of Life." One week, after the show's announcer had introduced the next number and the orchestra began to play, the canaries fell silent, refusing to sing a note. Convinced that the birds had lost their will to sing, the announcer stated, "During the next musical selection, the Hartz Mountain canaries will NOT be singing along." As soon as the music began, the canaries began to chirp louder than they had ever chirped before, much to the embarrassment of the red-faced announcer.

...The not-to-be-forgotten episode of the When A Girl Marries daytime drama serial, when the cast of the show, including the show's star Mary Jane Higby and actresses Rosemary Rice and Anne Burr, totally lost it, breaking up and laughing uncontrollably for over five minutes of live air time. What caused this breakup? Toward the end of the show, Rice, playing a young farmer's wife had said, "Yes, we've saved the potato crap," instead of "crop" and each line that followed, seemed more hysterical than the one before it to the actors as they tried to read their scripts. By the time the show ended, all that could be heard was the sound of women's laughter, as the flustered announcer tried to read the program's final commercial message.

Unexplainably, according to Higby not a single inquiry was made as to why the show had ended in such chaos, even though it was known to have had millions of loyal listeners.

"Goodnight...and Pleasant Dreams"

There were certainly other unforgettable moments that occurred during those glory days of radio...but, as with all days, sunset came, and the day came to an end. It was not forgotten. It becomes an important part of our past. And what a glorious past that was!

CHAPTER TEN

The Golden Age of Radio Lives On

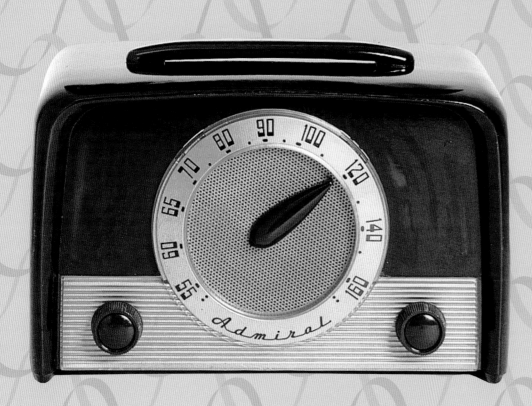

The Golden Age of Radio Lives On

Radio is Overshadowed by the Blue Glow of Television

Two years after World War II ended, the manufacture of products deemed "unessential to the war effort" resumed, and the public began to demand the "radio with pictures (TV)," they had been promised before the war began. Television had been one of the highlight exhibits at the pre-war 1939 New York World's Fair in Flushing Meadows, New York. Invented by Russian immigrant Vladamir Kosma Zworykin, who worked for the Westinghouse Company, television had been a very real possibility since 1929, when NBC president David Sarnoff began conducting numerous experiments. Sarnoff invested over 50 million dollars in Zworykin's invention, but the manufacture of television receivers cheap enough for the general public to afford, had to be postponed until the end of World War II. A booming post war economy and years of wartime savings enabled people to purchase newly produced, reasonably priced TV receivers and by 1947 Americans began to abandon radio for the joys of their new home entertainment toy---television. Unlike the people of other countries that saw no reason to discard the variety of programs radio had to offer to watch television, since both mediums could be enjoyed concurrently, the people of the U. S. turned off their radios and turned on their TV sets. By the early 1960's, when the last of the big network shows were cancelled, radio had been given over to endless hours of locally produced news, recorded music, and talk programs. Eventually, the major networks, feeling there was more money to be made from their television activities, gradually sold off their local radio stations one by one, and big time national radio was no more. It had passed into the genre of "nostalgia"

RCA's new TV sets are a highlight of the 1939 World's Fair

The Golden Age of Radio Lives On…

Despite the excitement over the coming of television, and the public fascination with "live pictures," the impact of Radio had been so very meaningful to many people. Many of the terms, references and phrases from radio shows and its stars had become common expressions. Many a mother admonished a child that their closet looked like it belonged to Fibber and Molly McGee. The phrases "Goodnight, Gracie," "Who's on first?", "The Shadow knows!" and "Your money or your life!" found their way into our daily conversations. People were running like "Gangbusters," asking each other for "just the facts, ma'am" and shouting "Hi-Yo, Silver!"

Radio was a "live" medium, often with so little preparation that it is inconceivable today. Radio brought us spontaneity and freshness that was simply irresistible and could never be replicated. Fortunately, many of those original broadcasts were preserved on transcription discs by sound engineers and in time transferred to tape. It has been estimated that there are several hundred thousand shows that have survived. Many of these have been made available on cassette and compact disc.

We do not have to wonder what Radio's Golden Age was all about.

We can experience it.

Program Notes

Disc I—Track One

Excerpts from:
When Radio Was Young

Inner Sanctum Opening
Walter Winchell
Jack Benny's Violin
Gangbusters
Fibber McGee's Closet
Abbott & Costello
Burns & Allen with Eddie Cantor
Jack Benny
Lights Out
The Shadow
The First Nighter
Lux Radio Theatre
Dragnet
Mr. District Attorney
Bing Crosby
Kate Smith
Superman
The Lone Ranger
Truth or Consequences
Information Please
Ma Perkins
Our Gal Sunday
Herbert Hoover
Warren G. Harding
Franklin D. Roosevelt
H. V. Kaltenborn
Harry Truman
Paul Whiteman Orchestra
Graham McNamee
Ted Husing
Clem McCarthy

Les Damon, left, barks an ultimatum to chagrined Walter Vaughn, right, while Roger de Koven stands by during a climactic sequence of "Gangbusters," veteran radio series heard every Saturday on CBS.

FDR

Truth or Consequence

Those three indomitable experts, Clifton Fadiman, Franklin P. Adams and John Kiernan, attempt to "stump" the nation's radio dialers every Tuesday evening on the "Information Please" program.

Bing Crosby

Jack Benny

Bergen, Mortimer Snerd and
Charlie McCarthy

Bud Abbott and Lou Costello's
debate, "Who's On First?"

Disc I-Track Two

Excerpts from:
Comedy's Golden Age

Ed Wynn as "The Fire Chief" jokes with Graham McNamee (1932-1935)
The Rudy Vallee Show with Joe Penner "Wanna buy a duck?" (1929-1945)
Amos 'n' Andy (Freeman Gosden and Charles Correll) buy a car from Kingfish (1929-1960)
The Eddie Cantor Show with Bert Gordon as "The Mad Russian" and guest star Jean Sablon
(1931-1949)
The Edgar Bergen/Charlie McCarthy Show: Bergen offers job to Mortimer Snerd after
Charlie resigns (1937-1956)
The Abbott and Costello Show: Bud and Lou debate "Who's On First?" (1942-1949)
Duffy's Tavern: Ed Gardner as "Archie The Manager" (1941-1952)
The Burns and Allen Show: Gracie reads a letter from her sister to George (1941-1949)
The Red Skelton Show: "Junior, the mean widdle kid" bluffs grandma and mom
(1941-1953)
The Jack Benny Show: Jack takes a violin lesson from "Professor" Mel Blanc and
visits the vault (1932-1955)
Bob Hope visits a Marine Base on Command Performance (1942-1949)
Will Rogers pokes fun at Congress (1933-1935)
Groucho Marx on "You Bet Your Life" kids around with guests (1947-1956)
Fibber McGee and Molly (Marian and Jim Jordan) are visited by Wally Wimple.
(1935-1956)
Baby Snooks (Fanny Brice) takes a piano lesson from Daddy (Hanley Stafford)
(1944-1951)
The Eddie Cantor Show: Eddie reviews his career with Harry Von Zell (1931-1949)
Jane and Goodman Ace, "Easy Aces," take a phone call (1932-1948)
Fred Allen goes down Allen's Alley with Senator Claghorn, Titus Moody and Mrs. Nussbaum
(1942-1949)

Ed Wynn

Groucho Marx

Fanny Brice as Baby Snooks

Disc 2-Track One

Excerpts from:
Voices of the 20th Century

FDR's First Inaugural Address
(March 4, 1933)
FDR's Fireside Chat
(March 12, 1933)
FDR's "Rendezvous with Destiny" speech
(June 27, 1936)
Chancellor Adolph Hitler of Germany
(1938)
Benito Mussolini, the Duce of Italy
Prime Minister Winston Churchill's "Finest Hour" Speech
(June 17, 1940)
Senator Huey Long of Louisiana
Mayor Fiorello LaGuardia of New York City
(July 1945)
Edward VIII's Abdication Speech
(December 11, 1936)
The Hindenburg Air Disaster reported by Herbert Morrison
(May 6, 1937)

Senator Huey Long

Disc 2-Track Two

Excerpts from:
Radio Coverage of World War II from Munich to
Hiroshima. (1938-1945)

The sudden tragic explosion of the "Hindenburg"

Mussolini Speaks, 1933

"The Adventures of Sherlock Holmes" with Basil Rathbone and Nigel Bruce
(1939-1946)

Disc 2 - Track Three

Excerpts From:
Drama: Theatre of the Mind

Suspense (1942-1962) Orson Welles in "The Hitchhiker"
Grand Central Station (1937-1954)
Charlie Chan (1932-1948)
The Romance of Helen Trent (1933-1960)
Academy Award Theatre (1946) Bogart, Astor and Greenstreet in "The Maltese Falcon"
Dragnet with Jack Webb (1949-1956)
Flash Gordon (1935-1936)
Suspense (1942-1962) Agnes Moorehead in "Sorry Wrong Number"
Lux Radio Theatre (1934-1955) with Katherine Hepburn and James Stewart in
"The Philadelphia Story"
X-Minus One (1955-1958)
Sherlock Holmes (1930-1955) with Basil Rathbone and Nigel Bruce
Gunsmoke (1952-1961)
The Whistler (1942-1955)
The Green Hornet (1936-1952)
Mary Noble, Backstage Wife (1935-1959)
I Love A Mystery (1939-1952) "The Temple of Vampires"
Just Plain Bill (1932-1955)
Tarzan (1932-1934)
The Fat Man (1946-1950)
Arch Oboler's Lights Out (1934-1943) "The Chicken Heart"
The Lone Ranger (1933-1955)
The Shadow (1930-1954)

The Romance of Helen Trent

Just Plain Bill

Bill Conrad (right), star of "Gunsmoke," conferring with producer-director
Norman Macdonnell during rehearsal

Disc 2 - Track Four

Excerpts From:
Collector's Gems

Mae West and Don Ameche play Adam and Eve in a saucy sketch that gets Ms. West banned from radio.
Marlon Brando in a scene from "A Streetcar Named Desire" in Brando's only dramatic appearance on radio.
Marilyn Monroe and Charlie McCarthy almost get married in Monroe's only radio appearance on radio ever.

Famous Sign-Offs

Ben Bernie
Eddie Cantor
Bob Hope
Fibber McGee and Molly
Jimmy Durante

W.C.Fields

Schwarzkopf directs **Gangbusters**
Colonel Norman H. Schwarzkopf, former superintendent of the New Jersey State Police and noted
criminal investigator, receiving instruction from Paul Monroe, CBS production man for "Gangbusters."

Bob Hope and Jerry Colonna

CBS radio microphone

NBC radio microphone

Agnes Moorehead was often called the "first lady of radio"

Jack Benny Program

Index

A

A&P Gypsies, The   4
A Date With Judy   26, 28
A Day In The Life Of Dennis Day   26
A Right To Happiness   37
A-1 Detective Agency   15
Abbott, Bud   20
Abbott and Costello Show, The   9, 20
Abie's Irish Rose   24
Ace, Goodman   26
Acuff, Roy   30
Adams, Mason   16, 37
Adams, Doc   18
Adams, Uncle Bill   32
Adams, Franklin P.   42
Adams, Harding Karen   37
Adventures of Ellery Queen, The   13
Adventures of Mr. and Mrs. North, The   13
Adventures of Philip Marlowe, The   13
Adventures of Bulldog Drummond, The   14
Adventures of Charlie Chan, The   13
Adventures of Dick Tracy, The   32
Adventures of Ozzie and Harriet, The   24
Adventures of Red Ryder, The   32
Adventures of Sam Spade, Detective, The   13
Adventures of Sherlock Holmes, The   13
Adventures of Superman, The   33
Adventures of the Thin Man, The   13
Aggie, Aunt   23
Al Pearce Show, The   21
Aldrich, Henry   24
Aldrich Family, The   24
Aley, Albert   32
Allen, Fred   20, 22
Allen, Barbara Jo   21
Allen, Gracie   25, 55
Allman, Elvia   21
Ameche, Jim   33
American Album of Familiar Music, The   30
America's Town Meeting of the Air   42
Amos 'n' Andy   ii, 5
Anderson, Eddie   22
Anderson, Marian   30
Anderson, Arthur   32
Andrew Sisters, The   21, 22, 30, 47

Appel, Anna   24
Arden, Eve   28
Arden and Gustave Haenschen Orchestra   30
Armed Forces Network   47
Armstrong, Edwin   2
Arnall, Curtis   40
Arnaz, Desi   28
Arnold, Eddy   30
Arquette, Cliff   27
Arthur Godfrey Time   36
Ascot, Rita   36
Ask-It-Basket   43
AT&T   3
Atwater, Mrs.   23
Auerbach, Artie   21
Austin, Gene   20
Author Meets the Critics   42
Autry, Gene   30

B

Babbitt, Harry   23
Baby Snooks   24
Bacall, Lauren   47
Backstage Wife   37, 40
Backus, Georgia   28
Baer, Parley   18
Bailey, Bob   28
Baker, Bonnie   30
Ball, Lucille   17, 28
Barbour, Henry   38
Barbour, Hazel   38
Barbour, Caludia   38
Barbour, Clifford   38
Barbour, Jack   38
Barbour, Family   38
Barker, Uncle   28
Barkley, Luise   37
Barletti, Julia   3
Barnes, Paul   33
Barney, Marion   40
Barrymore, Lionel   39
Baruch, Andre   30
Basco, Luigi   27
Basco, Rosa   27

Batman   33
Battle of Britain   46
Becker, Sandy   37
Beckett, Scotty   28
Beebee, Elsie   37
Beemer, Brace   34
Been, Bobbie   21
Begley, Ed   13
Bell, Alexander Graham   30
Bell, Ralph   16
Bell, Shirley   33
Bell Telephone Hour   30
Ben Bernie Show   30
Benaderet, Bea   22, 26, 27, 28
Bendix, William   28
Bennett, Constance   20
Bennett, Joan   20
Benny, Jack   ii, 20, 21, 22, 26
Bergen Edgar   ii, 21, 51
Berner, Sara   22
Best, Edna   27
Beulah   26
Bey, Turham   9
Big Town   13
Billsbury, Rye   33
Bing Crosby Show, The   30
Binyon, Conrad   28
Bird, Molly   38
Birdie   27
Bivens, Jack   33
Black Beauty   34
Blanc, Mel   22
Blondell, Gloria   28
Blondell, Brown   28
Blondie   24
Blue Network   7
Blurt, Elmer   21
Bob and Ray   37
Bob Hope Show, The   21
Bobby Benson and the B-Bar Riders   32
Bogart, Humphrey   39, 47
Bogue, Merwyn   23
Boles, Jim   15, 34
Booth, Shirley   26
Bordoni, Irene   4
Boston Blackie   14
Boswell Sisters   30

Botsford, Count Benchley   23
Bouchey, Bill   33
Bowen, Patsy   14
Bowes, Major Edward   24
Brandon, Ray   37
Brasfield, Rod   30
Break The Bank   43
Breakfast Club   36
Brice, Fanny   24
Brooks, Connie   28
Brown, John   26, 28
Brown, Ellen   37
Bryant, Arthur Q.   26, 27
Buck Rogers on the 25th Century   32
Buckingham Choir, The   30
Bumstead, Dagwood   24
Bunce, Alan   26, 37
Burdette, Winston   46
Burns, George   25, 55
Burns and Allen Show, The   25
Bushman, Francis X   38
Buttram, Pat   34

C

Can You Top This   42, 44
Caniff, Milton   33
Canova, Judy   23
Cantor, Eddie   21
Cantor, Charlie   24, 26
Captain Midnight   33
Carlyle, Louise   30
Carnation Contented Hour, The   30
Carnation Evaporated Milk   30
Carney, Art   16
Carney, Don   32
Carpenter, Cliff   33
Carroll Jr., Bob   28
Carter, Nick   9
Carter's Little Liver Pills   16
Casey, Crime Photographer   14
Cassidy, Ajax   22
Cavalcade of America   39
Chamber Music Society of Lower Basin Street   30
Chan, Charlie   13

Chandler, Jeff 28
Chandler, Robin 42
Chaney, Frances 33
Chappell, Ernest 14
Chase and Sanborne Hour With Edgar Bergen and Charlie McCarthy 21
Chesterfield Supper Club, The 30
Chestfield Cigarettes 30
Chichi 37
Christie, Ken 30
Cities Service Concerts, The 5
Claghorn, Senator 22
Clara, Lu and Em 36
Clark, Buddy 30
Cline, Patsy 30
Cliquot Club Eskimos, The 4
Clyde, Mr. 28
Colbert, Claudette 39
Cole, Alonzo Dean 15
Collins, Ray 39
Collyer, Bud 24, 33
Colonna, Jerry 21, 47
Columbia Workshop 47
Columbo, Russell 20
Command Performance 47
Como, Perry 30
Comstock, Bill 21
Conklin, Peggy 28
Conklin, Osgood 28
Connor, Nadine 24
Conrad, Dr. Frank 3
Conrad, William 18
Conried, Hans 23, 27, 28
Coogan, Richard 24
Cook, Tommy 28
Coons, Johnny 28
Coppin, Grace 28
Corbett, Lois 26
Corkin, Flip 33
Corliss, Fuffy 28
Correl, Charles 5
Corwin, Norman ii, iii, 47
Costello, Lou 20
Cotsworth, Staats 14
Coty Program, The 4
Cranston, Lamont 12
Crenna, Richard 28

Cresta Blanca Carnival and Lucky Strike Program 23
Cromwell, Richard 38
Cronkite, Walter 46
Crosby, Bing 5, 20, 30, 47
Cross, Milton 4
Crumit, Frank 4
Crunchmuller, Joe 23
Cumberland Moutain Boys 30
Curtin, Joseph 37

D

Daley, Cass 47
Dallas, Stella 37
Damerel, Donna 37
Dandridge, Ruby 23
Dane, Donald 30
Dark, Victory 39
Davidson, Bill 37
Davis, Dix 26
Davis, Mrs. 28
Davis, Beryl 30
Davis, Gwen 32
Davis, Joan 36
Davis, Bette 20, 39, 47
Davis, Elmer 46
Day, Dennis iii, 22, 26
Day, Doris 30
De Forest, Lee 2, 46
de Haviland, Olivia 17
Deanes, Martha 43
DeCamp, Rosemary 39
de Corsia, Ted 33
De Leath, Vaughn 4
Delmar, Kenny 22, 39
DeMarco Sisters 22
DeMille, Cecil B. 39
Denney, George V. 42
Denning, Richard 28
Denton, Walter 28
Devine, Andy 27
Dickenson, Jean 30
Dillon, U.S Marshall Matt 18
Dollar, Johnny 15

Don McNeils Breakfast Club 26
Don Winslow of the Navy 32
Donald, Peter 22
Dorothy and Dick 36
Double or Nothing 43
Douglas, Sharon 28
Douglas, Susan 36
Doyle, D.A. Len 14
Dr. Christian 39, 40
Dr. I.Q. 43
Dracula 39
Dragnet 15
Dragon Lady 33
Dryden, Robert 16
Duffy, Miss 26
Duffy's Tavern 26
Dunlap, Patricia 37
Durante, Jimmy 23, 47
Durante Moore Show, The 23
Durbin, Deanna 21
Duskin, Ruthie 42

E

Earhart, Amelia 43
Easy Aces 26
Ed Wynn Show, The 3
Eddie Cantor Show, The 21
Eddy, Nelson 30
Edwards, Sam 28
Edwards, Joan 30
Edwards, Ralph 43
Egleston, Charles 36
Eiler, Barbara 28
Einstein, Harry 21
Ellen, Minette 38
Elliot, Bob 37
Ellis, Georgia 18
Ellis, Dellie 26
Eloise, Kummer 37
Elstner, Anne 37
Engel, Roy 33
Eric, Elspeth 16
Erickson, Louise 26, 27
Escape 14

Ethel and Albert 26
Evans, Dale 21, 34
Eveready Hour, The 5

F

Fadiman, Clifton 42
Fairbanks, Douglas 20
Faith, Percy 30
Falkenburg, Jinx 36
Famous Jury Trials 14
Faraday, Michael 2
Farrar, Stanley 26
Fat Man, The 15
Faust, Donovan 34
FBI in Peace and War, The 14
Felton, Verna 23
Fennelley, Parker 22
Fessenden, Reginald Aubrey 2
Fibber McGee and Molly iii, iv, 26, 27
Fidler, Jimmy 42
Fields, W.C. 21, 51
Fifi, Madamioselle 21
Fillbrandt, Laurette 36
Finnegan 26
Fire Chief, The 3
Fireside Chats 46
First Nighter Program 39
Fitzgerald, Ed 36
Fitzgerald, Pegeen 36
Fleischmann's Hour, The 5
Fleming, Sir Ambrose 2
Fletcher, Uncle 28
Fletcher, Vincent 30
Fletcher Markie's Studio One 39
Flynn, Charles 33
Foley, Red 30
Fontaine, Frank 21
Ford, Ed 42
Ford Theater 39
Forte, Joe 27
Foster, Judy 26
Foster Dr. Leslie 38
Frances, Ada 3
Francis, Arlene 30, 42

Frank Black Orchestras 30
Franklin, Dexter 28
Fred Allen Show The 22
Fred Waring and His Pennsylvanian's 30
Freeman, Florence 37
Friday "Sergeant Joe" 15
Fridell, Vivian 37

G

Gable, Martin 39
Gable, Clark 39, 47
Gaerson, Betty Lou 37
Gamble, Doc 26
Gangbusters 16
Garde, Betty 37
Gardner, Ed (Archie) 26
Garland, Judy 21, 30, 39, 47
Gene Autry Show 18
General Electric 3, 7
Geranium 23
Gershwin, George 3
Gibbs, Georgia 30
Gibson, John 14
Gilbert, Jody 27
Gildersleeve, Throckmorton P. 26, 27
Gillars, Mildred 46
Gillis, Ann 26
Gill's Orchestra 3
Gilman, Page 38
Girl Intern 37
Gleason, Jackie 28
Goff, Norris 27
Good News 24
Goodmann, Alice 21
Goodmann, Al 24, 30
Goodmann, Gordon 30
Goodwin, Eve 27
Gook, Vickie 28
Gook, Sade 28
Gook, Rush 28
Gordon, Anita 21
Gordon, Bert 21
Gordon, Gale 26, 28
Gordon, Gloria 28

Gosden, Freeman 5
Gothard, David 36, 37, 40
Goulding, Raymond 37
Grable, Betty 17, 39, 47
Grand Central Station 39
Grand Ole Opry, The 30
Great Expectations 39
Great Gildersleeve, The 26, 27
Green, Marie 21
Green, Rosaline 24
Green, Eddie 26
Green, Rosaline 30
Green, Marie 30
Green, Johnny 30
Green Hornet, The 33, 34
Grey, Nan 38
Griffin, Ken 37
Grimes, Jack 28, 32
Guiding Light, The 37
Gumpox, Jake 28
Gunsmoke ii, 18

H

Haines, Larry 16
Hall, Cliff 23
Hall, Bob 34
Hamilton, Steve 37
Hammett, Dashiell 15
Happiness Boys, The 4
Harding, Warren 3
Harris, Arlene 21, 24
Harris, Phil 22
Harris, Stacy 33
Hartz Mountain Canaries, The 52, 30
Hartzell, Clarence 28
Hayes, George "Gabby" 34
Hayton, Lennie 30
Hayworth, Rita 17, 39
Heatter, Gabriel 46
Heller, Little Jackie 30
Hemingway, Mr. 23
Henning, Arthur Sears 9
Henry, Joseph 2
Henry, Captain 24

Henry, Bill 38
Hershfield, Harry 42
Hersholt, Gene 39
Hertz, Hendrich 2
Higby, Mary Jane 36, 52
Himber, Richard 30
Hindenburg 50
Hiroshima 48
Hodge, Al 34
Hogan, Snake 27
Holbrook, John 37
Hollywood Hotel 20
Honey and the Bees 30
Honeybee 28
Honeywell, Oliver 27
Hoover, Herbert 3
Hop, Harrigan 32
Hope, Bob 21, 30, 47
Horne, Lena 30
Hottelet, Richard C. 46
Hour Of Charm 30
Howard, Tom 42, 44
Howe, Quincy 46
Huddleston, Dick 27
Hughes, Arthur 14
Hughes, David 28
Hughes, Donald 32
Hughes, Arthur 37, 40
Hughes, Charles Evan 46
Human Chatter Box Pearce, The 21
Hurt, Marlin 26

I

I Love A Mystery ii, 15
I Love Lucy 28
Idelson, Billy 28
Information Please 42, 44
Inner Sanctum Mysteries 16
Interwoven Pair, The 4
Ish Kabibble 23
It Happened One Night 39
It Pays To Be Ignorant 42
It's A Wonderful Life 39

J

Jack Armstrong the All American Boy 33
Jack Benny Program, The 22
Jackson, Jay 43
Jamison, Anne 20
Jimmy Durante Show, The 23
John's Other Wife 37
Johnson, Edward ii
Johnson, Raymond Edward 16, 30
Johnson Wax Company 26
Jolson, Al 30
Jones, Grandpa 30
Jordan, Jim 17, 26
Jordan, Marian 17, 26
Jordan, Owen 33
Jordan, Joyce 37
Joseph Horne Company Department Store 3
Jostyn, Jay 14
Judy Canova Show 23
Jungle, Jim 32
Just Plain Bill 37, 40

K

Kalish, Scheindel 16
Kaltenborn, H.V. 46
Kate Smith Show, The 20, 30
Kate Smith Speaks 30
Kay Kyser's Kollege of Musical Knowledge 23
KDKA 2, 3
Kearns, Joseph 23, 26
Keighley, William 39
Kelk, Jackie 33
Kelly, Joe 42
Kent, Clark 33
Kiernan, John 42
Kildare, Dr. Leslie 38
Kilgallen, Dorothy 36
King, John Reed 43
King Sisters 21
Kinsella, Walter 24
Kirkpatrick, Jess 30
Kitzel, Mr. 21

Klein, Evelyn Kaye 30
Klein, Adelaide 33
Knight, Evelyn 30
Knight, Fuzzy 34
Kollmar, Richard 14, 36
Kraft Music Hall, The 30
Kramer Nelson, Carolyn 37
Kropotkin, Professor 28
Kross, Sid 28
Kruger, Alma 38
Kupperman, Joel 42
Kyser, Kay 23
KYW 3

L

La Curto, Jack 12
Lady Vere-de-vere 26
LaGuardia, Fiorella H. 51
Laine, Frankie 30
Lake, Arthur 24
Lambert, Scrappy 30
Lane, Margot 12
Langford, Frances 20, 21
Lanny Ross Show, The 30
Larrimore, Earl 37
Latimer, Ed 40
LaTrivia, Mayor 26
Laughing Lady 21
Lauck Chester 27
Laughton, Charles 17
Laurie Jr., Joe 42
Lawrence, Bill 30
Lazer, Joan 32
Lesueur, Larry 46
Ledoux, Lenore 24
Lee, Peggy 21, 30
Lee, Barbara 30
LeGrand, Richard 27
Lennox, Eleanor 30
Leonard, Sheldon 23
Lester, Jack 33
Let's Pretend 32
Levy, Abie 24
Levy, Solomon 24

Lewis, Elliott ii
Lewis, Cathy 27
Lewis, Forrest 27, 34
Life of Riley, The 28
Life Saver Candy Company 9
Life with Luigi 27
Lights Out 14
Lipton, Bill 32
Lipton Tea 16
Liss, Ronald 33
Little French Princess, The 36
Little Orphan Annie 33, 51
Livingston, Mary 22
Locke, Ralph 37
Lone Ranger, The iii, 9, 18, 30, 34
Long, Doc 15
Lord, Phillips H. 16
Lorenzo, Jones 37
Lucas, George iii
Lucky Strike 22
Luddy, Barbara 39
Lum and Abner 27
Lux Radio Theater, The iv, 39
Lynch, Peg 26
Lynn, Diana 28
Lynn, Loretta 30
Lyon, Priscilla 28

M

Ma Perkins 36
Macdonnell, Norman ii, 18
McGrath, Paul 16
Mack, Helen 28
Mack, Nila 32
Mad Russian, The 21
Major Bowes and His Original Amateur Hour 24
Malone, Pick 24
Malone, Jerry 37
Maltin, Leonard iii
Manson, Charlotte 14
March of Time, The 39
Marconi, Senetore Guglielmo 2
Mardi Gras 30

Marsh, Myra 26
Marshall, John 38
Martha Dean Show, The 43
Marx, Groucho 54
Matthews, Dr. Charles 37
Maxwell, James Clerk 2
Maxwell, Marilyn 21
Maxwell House Coffee 24
Mayfield, Aunt Emily 38
Mayor of the Town 39
MBS (Mutual Radio Network) 9
McBride, Mary Margaret 43, 44
McCambridge, Mercedes 16, 24, 37
McCammon, Bess 36
McCarthy, Charlie ii, 21, 51
McCarthy, Jack 34
McClain, Jimmy 43
McConnell, Lulu 42, 44
McCormick, Myron 16
McCrarey, Tex 36
McDaniel, Hattie 24
McElhone, Eloise 42
McGregor, Evelyn 30
McLaughlin, Don 36
McLaughton, Harry 42, 44
McNear, Howard 18
McNeill, Don 36
McNellis, Maggie 42
Meet Corliss Archer 28
Meet Millie 28
Meet The Press 42
Meighan, James 37
Melody Ranch 34
Melton, James 30
Mercer, Johnny 47
Mercury Theater 51
Mercury Theater of the Air, The 39
Merman, Ethel 47
Miller, Doc 27
Mills Brothers 30
Miner, Jan 14
Miranda, Carmen 47
Mitchell, Shirley 27
Modernaires, The 30
Molasses and January 24
Mollé Mystery Theater, The 14
Moody, Titus 22

Moore, Grace 30
Moorehead, Agnes ii, 33, 39
Morgan, Janet 28
Morgan, Claudia 37
Morgan, Frank 47
Morrison, Brett 12, 30, 39
Morrison, Herb 50
Morse, Carlton ii, 15, 38, 40
Mostel, Zero 30
Mr. Chameleon 14
Mr. District Attorney 14
Mr. Keen, Tracer of Lost Persons 14
Mullen, Frank 2
Munchhausen, Baron 23
Munn, Frank 30
Murphy, Rosemary 24
Murphy, Patrick 24
Murrow, Edward R. 46
My Favorite Husband 28
My Friend Irma 28
My Man Godfrey 39
Mysterious Traveler, The 14

N

Naish J. Carrol 27
Neisen, Gertrude 20
Nelson, Frank 22
Nelson, Ozzie 24
Nelson, Willie 30
Nichols, Anne 24
Nick Carter, Master Detective 14
Nightingdale, Earl 33
Noble, Edward J. 7, 9
Noble, Mary 37
Noble, Larry 37
Nolan, Jeanette ii
Nolan, Bob 34
Nussbaum, Pansy 22

O

Obese, Pasqual — 27
Oboler, Arch — ii, 14
O'Day, Michael — 32
O'Dell, Digger — 28
Omar, General — 43
One Man's Family — 38
O'Neil, Kitty — 21
Ortega, Santos — 16
Our Gal Sunday — 36
Our Miss Brooks — 28

P

Packard P.I., Jack — 15
Packard Hour, The — 30
Padgett, Pat — 24
Paley, William S. — 6, 8
Palmolive Beauty Box Show, The — 5
Palmolive Brushless Shaving Cream — 16
Parker, Frank — 20
Parker, Jennison — 21
Parsons, Louella — 20
Parties at Pickfair — 20
Pasternack, Josef — 30
Paterson, Walter — 15
Patton, Alice — 37
Paul, Les — 30
Payne, Virginia — 36
Peabody, Grandpappy — 27
Pearl, Jack — 23
Pearl, Minnie — 30
Pearl Harbor — 46, 48
Ped Pipers — 30
Peeples, Cornelius — 27
Peery, Hal — 26
Peevey, Floyd the Barber — 27
Pepper Young's Family — 37
Perrott, Ruth — 23
Peters, Ken — 27
Peterson, Irma — 28
Peterson, Arthur — 37
Pickens, Janet — 30

Pickford, Mary — 20
Pious, Minerva — 22
Pitts, Zasu — 27
Pittsburgh Community Chorus — 3
Pittsburgh Sun, The — 3
Pons, Lily — 30
Popeye the Sailor — 32
Portia Faces Life — 37
Powell, William S. — 20
Powell, Dick — 20
Prentiss, Ed — 33
Price, Vincent — 14
Pritchett, Florence — 42
Proudfoot, Chester — 18
Pugh, Madelyn — 28

Q

Quiet Please — 14
Quiz Kids, The — 42

R

Raby, John — 52
Raffetto, Michael — 15, 38
Raht, Jameson — 24
Raht, Katherine — 24
Randall, Tony — 15
Randolph, Isabel — 26
Randolph, Lillian — 27
Ransom, Lilah — 27
RCA — 3, 7
Readick, Bob — 32
Red Network — 7
Reed, Alan — 21, 24, 26, 27, 28
Reid, Britt — 34
Reinheart, Alice — 16, 37
Reis, Irving — iii
Rice, Howard — 32
Rice, Rosemary — 52
Rich, Freddie — 30
Richard Diamond Private Detective — 13
Riker, Ernie — 36

Riley, Babs — 28
Riley, Junior — 28
RKO Hour, The — 4
Robespierre — 24
Robinson, Larry — 32
Rochester — 22
Rogers, Will — 4, 5
Rogers, Roy — 18
Romance of Helen Trent, The — 36, 40
Rose, Tokyo — 46
Roseleigh, Jack — 40
Roosevelt, Franklin Delano — 46, 48
Ross, Lanny — 24, 30
Roy Rogers Show, The — 34
Runyon P.I., Brad — 15
Russell, Andy — 30
Russell, Ruth — 40
Ruthledge, Mary — 37
Rutledge, Dr. John — 37
Ryan, Patricia — 32, 33

S

Saint, The — 14
Sally, Axis — 46
Sanderson, Julia — 4
Sarnoff, David — 6, 7, 54
Saturday Night Serenade — 5
Sanders, Lugene — 28
Sayao, Bidu — 30
Schultz, Horowitz — 27
Schwarzkopf, Colonel H. Norman — 16
Sea Hound, The — 32
Sergeant Preston of the Yukon — iii
Sevareid, Eric — 46
Shadow, The — iv, 9, 12, 16, 54
Shaw, Hollace — 30
Shelton, George — 42, 44
Shephard, Ann — 16
Shields, Fred — 28
Shore, Dinah — 21, 30, 47
Showboat — 24
Shirer, William L. — 46
Silver — 34
Simms, Ginny — 23, 47

Sinatra, Frank — 5, 30, 47
Singing Lady, The — 32
Singleton, Penny — 24
Sivony, L.C. — 21
Sky King — 33
Slater, Bill — 43
Sloane, Everett — 16, 39
Small, Mary — 30
Smart, J. Scott — 15
Smelly Clark — 28
Smith, Katherine — 30
Smith, Howard K. — 46
Smolen, Vivian — 37
Smythe, J. Anthony — 38
Snerd, Mortimer — 21
Solomon, Papa David — 37
Soubier, Cliff — 33
Soule, Olan — 39
Spade, Sam — ii
Spier, Sam — 17
Spitalny, Phil — 30
Squire Skimp — 27
Stacy, Jane — 28
Stafford, Hanley — 24
Stafford, Jo — 30
Stalin, Jospeh — 48
Stander, Lionel — 21
Star Wars — iii
Stembottom, Ruthie — 28
Sterienzi, Lottie — 28
Stevens, Julie — 24, 36
Stewart, Blanche — 21
Stewart, James — 39
Stordahl, Axel — 30
Story of Myrt and Marge, The — 37
Straight Arrow — 32
Striker, Fran — 34
Studebaker, Hugh — 37
Superman — 33
Suspense — iv, 16, 17
Swarthout, Gladys — 30
Sweet Marion — 33
Swenson, Karl — 14, 16, 37

T

Tarplin, Maurice	14
Tarzan	32
Ted Fio Rita	20
Tedrow, Irene	28
Terry and the Pirates	33
Tetley, Walter	27
Tex and Jinx	36
Texaco Oil Company	3
Theater Guild on the Air, The	39
Thin Man, The	39
This Is Your FBI	15
Thomas, Lowell	46
Thorson, Russell	15
Those We Love	38
Tibbett, Lawrence	30
Tish, Lizzie	21
To The Girls	42
Todd, John	34
Tonto	34
Toscanini, Arturo	iii
Totter, Audrey	28
Tracy, Dick	47
Traubel, Helen	30
Tremayne, Les	39
Trendle, George W.	34
Trent, Sybil	32
Trigger	34
Trio, Buddy Weed	30
Trotter, John Scott	30
Truth or Consequence	43
Tubbs, Ernest	30
Tucker, Orrin	30
Turner, Lana	17, 39, 47
Tuttle, Lurene	ii, 27
Twenty Questions	43
Tyrell, St. John	33

U

U.S. Steel	39
Uncle Don	32, 51
Uppington, Mrs.	26

V

Vague Vera	21
Vail, Myrtle	37
Vail, Mert	37
Vainrib,Stanley	43
Valentine, Lew	43
Vallee, Rudy	4, 5
Vanda, Charles	17
Vaughn, Beryl	33
Vic and Sade	28
Vola, Vickie	14
Vonn, Veola	21
Voorhees, Donald	24, 30

W

Wain, Bea	30
Waldo, Janet	28
Wall, Lucille	37
Wallington, Jimmy	30
War Of The Worlds, The	39, 50
Warbucks, Daddy	33
Ward, Red	3
Waring, Fred	30
Warner, Gertrude	12
Waterman, Willard	37
WBZ	3
Wearybottom, Mrs.	26
Webb, Jack	15
Welles, Orson	iii, 12, 16, 39, 50
Wells, H.G.	39, 50
West, Mae	21
Westinghouse	3, 54
Wever, Ned	14
WGN	9
What A Life	24
When A Girl Marries	36, 52
Whiteman, Paul	3
Whiteman, Alfred	24
Whiting, Margaret	21
Whiting, Barbara	28
Widmark, Richard	16
Wilcox, Harlow	26

Wildon, Ward	42
Will Lustrin Orchestra	30
Williams, Ann	14
Williams, Hank	30
Wilson, Don	22
Wilson, Marie	28
Wilson, Janet	30
Wilson, Charlotte	37
Winchell, Walter	42, 48
Winkler, Betty	24
Winninger, Charles	24
Winslow, Paula	28
Wislon, Eileen	30
Witch's Tale	15
Wizard of Oz, The	39
WJZ	3, 4, 34
WLW	9
Wolfe, Miriam	15, 32
Woman In White , The	37
Woods, Donald	38
WOR	9, 43
World War II	10, 46, 54
Wragge, Betty	37, 40
WWJ	3
WXYZ	9
Wynn Ed	3, 20

Y

Yahbut	21
Yalta	48
Yarborough, Barton	15, 38
York, Dick	33
Yorke, Reggie	15
You Are There	39
Young Doctor Malone	37
Young Widder (Widow) Brown	37
Your Hit Parade	30
Yours Truly, Johnny Dollar	15

Z

Ziegfeld Follies, The	4, 5, 24
Zuckert, Bill	16
Zworykin, Vladamir Kosma	54